DATE DUE

			PRINTED IN U.S.A.

The Illustrated Guide to
ORNAMENTAL
SHRUBS

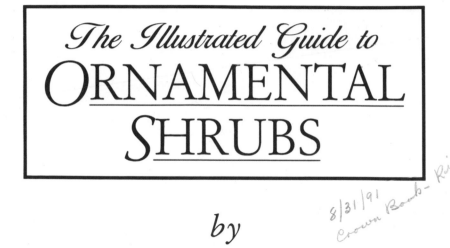

The Illustrated Guide to
ORNAMENTAL
SHRUBS

by
JAN TYKAČ

Illustrated by
ANNA SKOUMALOVÁ &
DANIELA TOUŠOVÁ

CHARTWELL
BOOKS, INC.

This 1990 edition

Published by

CHARTWELL BOOKS, INC.
A Division of **BOOK SALES, INC.**
110 Enterprise Avenue
Secaucus, New Jersey 07094

By arrangement with Octopus Books Limited
Copyright © 1990, Artia, Prague
ISBN 1 55521 652 8
Printed in Czechoslovakia by Svoboda, Prague
3/15/23/51-01

CONTENTS

Foreword   6

Variety and form   7

Siting shrubs correctly   8

Planting   10

Care and maintenance   11

Pruning   12

Propagating ornamental shrubs   14

Specimen shrubs   18

Informal hedges   20

Formal hedges   22

Groundcover shrubs   23

Shrubs in containers   24

Shrubs for a rock garden   25

Colour plates   27

Index   220

FOREWORD

Ornamental shrubs play a vital role in every garden. Just compare a dormant shrub with one in mid-summer, or its vivid greenery with its spectacular autumnal beauty, and the distinction between the seasons becomes obvious.

Now town house gardens are alloted less and less space, trees such as limes, poplars and weeping willows are far too large for them. So, lack of space has helped encourage the widest use of ornamental shrubs. Like trees, they help create good proportions in a garden and link it with the surrounding landscape.

Ornamental shrubs are long-lived, with woody stems and roots. They are generally shorter than trees, branching from the base without a main trunk. Mature shrubs flower every year and in favourable conditions bear fruits as well. But it is difficult to decide whether some plants are shrubs or trees, since there are transitional forms that make tree-like shrubs and some shrubby ornamentals are commonly grown on a trunk.

Ornamental shrubs are said to turn a plot of ground into a garden. They are also important in creating a clean environment in the garden in these times of widespread atmospheric pollution. A screen of ornamental shrubs planted along a boundary fence creates shelter, radically canging the garden's microclimate. Dense shrub planting reduces the noise coming from the streets outside and also keeps out much dust. Shrubs planted right round the periphery of the garden serve to create the feeling of intimacy we look for and help conceal unattractive buildings or fill undesirable gaps. They can also be planted to form an ornamental screen between the main garden and the compost heap, tool shed or vegetable plot.

In recent decades ornamental shrubs have been widely used to provide ground cover. Thickly planted ground cover saves labour by reducing weed growth. Sprigs of most ornamental shrubs are suitable for flower arranging in the home. It is a great pleasure to force sprigs indoors to create an impressive display of blossom in early spring, or even in winter, when flowers are sparse.

When choosing ornamental shrubs for the garden, select a range of shapes and colours for every season of the year to create a really interesting garden. Native shrubs are most suitable for country gardens, but in towns exotic kinds can be used. Be careful though when planting conspicuous species or forms like red-leaved maples or silver spruces, especially in gardens that merge with the surrounding landscape. But do not let this stop you from planting species with attractively coloured autumn foliage or fruits, which make a colourful exclamation point at the end of the growing season.

The pictorial section of this book illustrates a wide assortment of ornamental shrubs to satisfy even the most demanding gardeners.

Special attention has been given to species and cultivars with modest requirements that can be propagated easily by amateurs.

VARIETY AND FORM

The natural shape and eventual size of ornamental shrubs are the main points of interest to gardeners. Some shrubs have such conspicuous shapes that they can be easily recognized at a considerable distance.

The species itself can form a conical, cylindrical, oval or irregular-shaped head, or some intermediate shapes. Some species have given rise to garden forms with different-shaped heads from their parents, for instance, pendulous heads, usually named 'Pendula' or 'Inversa'. Pendulous forms can be grown to good effect on a tall slender trunk, as for example, some species of cotoneaster and robinia. Also atypical is a spherical head. Thickly-branched, slow-growing garden forms with spherical heads are generally named 'Globosa' or 'Compacta', among them being cultivars of cinquefoil (*Potentilla*), holly (*Ilex*) and spindle tree (*Euonymus*). Bizarre forms with twisted or contorted branches are called 'Monstrosa', 'Contorta' or 'Tortuosa', of which the most widely grown are forms of hazel (*Corylus*) and willow (*Salix*). 'Columnaris' and 'Fastigiata' indicate columnar forms of maple (*Acer*), hornbeam (*Carpinus*) and elm (*Ulmus*). Dwarf forms are gene-

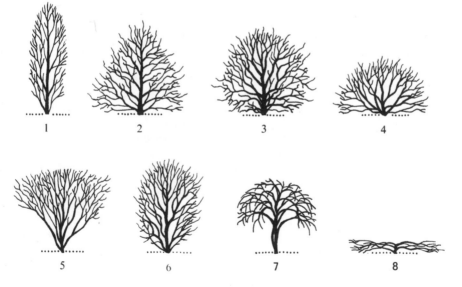

Shapes of ornamental shrubs: columnar (1), conical (2), spherical (3), hemispherical (4), funnel-shaped (5), oval (6), with arching branches (7), prostrate (creeping) (8).

rally named 'Nana'. Being slow growers they can be used to good effect even in very small gardens. Their increasing popularity has encouraged the production of many new forms.

The final size of a mature shrub is another important distinctive feature. Some ornamental woody plants, like the mock orange (*Philadelphus*), spiraea and honeysuckle (*Lonicera*), grow rapidly, reaching full size within a few years. Others grow slowly, especially when young, taking several decades to reach full size. These include tree peonies (*Paeonia*), magnolias and dwarf maples (*Acer*). The height of ornamental shrubs also greatly depends on the soil and climatic conditions of the garden.

Another key feature of every shrub is its texture, i. e. how its leaves and branchlets are arranged over its head. These three features — shape, size and texture — together constitute the habit of the shrub. Most ornamental shrubs make concentric growth, with the main branches growing from a single point at soil level. Some shrubs produce plenty of underground suckers, forming whole thickets from a single stem over several years.

These various features, together with the shrub's requirements as to soil and siting, determine the way it should be used and cared for in the garden.

SITING SHRUBS CORRECTLY

Selecting the right shrubs for a particular site is vital for success. Undemanding species can stand quite harsh conditions, but they can become unattractive and start to deteriorate, so their appearance does not satisfy their owner. We use the terms macroclimate and microclimate to describe garden conditions. Macroclimate is the climate of a large area that is beyond the influence of man. Microclimate, on the other hand, is the range of conditions in a limited area like a garden or part of it. It is shaped by the slope of the garden, how much of it is built on, the thickness of planting and the nearness of the sea or other large sheet of water. Temperatures in a town or city can be somewhat higher than in open country.

Naturally, plants are exposed to different conditions in the lowlands or high in the mountains, so height above sea level greatly affects the selection of shrubs for a particular location, since it helps dictate the average temperature, as well as the amount of rainfall and its distribution over the year.

Another factor in choosing shrubs for your garden is its distance from the equator. This determines the number of daylight hours, the intensity of the sunlight, the average temperature of the place, and the timing of the first autumn frosts and the last black frosts of spring, which mark the growing season for most plants.

The proximity of the sea or other large sheet of water also influences the climatic conditions in the garden. Many species will only succeed in a temperate maritime climate, while others can stand harsher continental conditions. Species that originated in maritime regions generally need high air humidity to succeed — evergreen shrubs at least 60% — and consequently, require shelter from wind.

Avoid frost pockets when planting tender species. These are depressions in which cold air accumulates, forcing the night temperature lower than elsewhere nearby. As cold air always sinks to the ground, this can occur in quite small hollows as well as in a larger enclosed sunken garden.

Most evergreen shrubs resent draughts, which increase the evaporation of water. A thick cover of snow protects plants from drying winter winds and prevents the soil from becoming too deeply frostbound. Damage by black frosts — those unaccompanied by snow — can be prevented by protecting the soil over the shrubs' roots with a layer of peat, dry foliage, composted pine bark or green brushwood and covering the top growth with straw held in place with plastic mesh. If very wet soil freezes around a shrub it can kill the plant by freezing its living tissues at soil level, so improve drainage where necessary. Work sharp sand or weathered ashes into the soil or carry surface water away in shingle-filled channels.

Some shrubs may fail to establish in the garden because of the wide-spreading shallow roots of neighbouring birches, hornbeams, chestnuts, maples and alders. But many shade-loving shrubs can be grown under deep-rooted trees such as oaks, ashes, larches and pines.

Delicate species cannot stand direct midday sun, particularly in late winter and early spring. The sun's rays reflected from a south-facing wall encourage the sap to rise too early and the precocious growth can often be damaged by black frosts. So tender species are best planted where a house or arbour casts its midday shadow over them providing natural shelter. Shrubs planted in the open should at least be protected with a piece of sacking attached to a frame.

Most shrubs thrive in any reasonably deep, nourishing garden soil. Native plants generally do well in less favourable conditions than introduced species. The poorer the soil and the harsher the climate, the more limited will be the choice of shrubs for your garden.

Shrubs that thrive in the sun are generally happy in a drier soil than shade-lovers. These sun-lovers include viburnums, forsythias and deutzias. The shade-lovers are mostly low-growing shrubs planted as undergrowth beneath taller trees. Lime content is another important point in cultivation. Lime-loving plants (calcicoles) include: barberry (*Berberis*), Judas tree (*Cercis*), Californian lilac (*Ceanothus*), smoke bush (*Cotinus*) and oleaster (*Elaeagnus*). Lime-haters (calcifuges) include rhododendrons, halesias, mezereons (*Daphne*), hydrangeas, witch hazels (*Hamamelis*), brooms (*Cytisus*) and magnolias.

Polluted air in a town or industrial area can also bring failure.

9

Shrubs that are reasonably tolerant of atmospheric pollution include dogwood (*Cornus*), hazel (*Corylus*), hawthorn (*Crataegus*), mezereon (*Daphne*), deutzia, oleaster (*Elaeagnus*), spindle tree (*Euonymus*), forsythia, witch hazel (*Hamamelis*), sea buckthorn (*Hippophaë*), hydrangea, kerria, laburnum, privet (*Ligustrum*), Chinese box thorn (*Lycium*), magnolia, mock orange (*Philadelphus*), roses, brooms (*Cytisus*), common elder (*Sambucus*), spiraea, lilac (*Syringa*) and viburnum.

PLANTING

Deciduous ornamental shrubs are planted when they are dormant, whenever the ground is free of frost and not excessively wet and airless. They are best planted after their leaves have been shed (October or early November), or in early spring (March to April). Early autumn planting is certainly preferable, as there is then a wide choice of lifted open-ground plants. Warm soil encourages young roots which absorb water to develop, so do not delay too long. Frost-bound soil causes the plant to wilt and die. Moreover, shrubs planted in autumn make new growth more rapidly and produce more flowers than those planted in spring.

Tender species such as magnolia, witch hazel (*Hamamelis*), rose mallow (*Hibiscus*) and buddleia are better planted in spring to avoid frost damage. If possible, hypericums, kolkwitzias, syringas and birches should also be planted in spring when the buds open. Water regularly after spring planting, for dry periods usually follow.

Container-grown plants with a well-developed rootball can be planted at any time of year, provided the soil and weather conditions are suitable. Avoid planting in winter when the soil is sodden or frost-bound and in midsummer when there may be a shortage of water.

Transplanting is a shock to any plant, but young plants generally recover more rapidly than old ones. Always try to plant the shrubs in their permanent position as quickly as possible. Bare-rooted plants should never be exposed to sunlight or frost. It is better to heel them in temporarily in a shady spot, so they do not dry out.

Before planting, dig the ground one spit deep (the depth of a spade blade), (30—50 cm / 12—20 in), mixing in garden compost or peat, for the plants will remain in the same place for many years. Be sure to remove all persistent weeds, which would otherwise become very troublesome later.

Cut back damaged roots or stems and pare the wounds clean with a sharp knife to speed healing. Always preserve as many roots as possible. Cut back hard species that flower in summer and autumn, like buddleias and hydrangeas. Woody plants with terminal buds are better not pruned — maples, aralias and magnolias, for example.

The size of the planting hole depends on the dimensions of the root ball, but if the soil is well-worked it need not be too deep. When

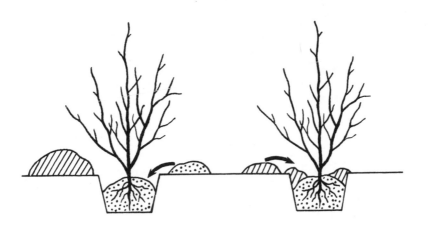

Planting ornamental shrubs (put nourishing soil around the roots).

planting a group of shrubs, the soil from the second hole can be used to fill in the first, and so on. If necessary, add a shovelful of well-rotted compost to the bottom of the hole. Plunge the roots in water to give them a good soak before planting.

Plant each shrub at the same depth as it grew in the nursery. The collar, where roots and stem join, should be about 5 cm (2 in) beneath the soil, as this will settle a little after watering. When planting, jiggle the shrub about to fill any air pockets around the roots. Tread the soil down firmly around the plant and water it liberally to bring the fine roots in close contact with the soil. Shape the soil around large specimen shrubs and trees to form a bowl for watering during summer droughts.

Evergreen shrubs should be planted in September and early October or in April. Before planting, plunge the plant in its container in water to soak the root ball. Then take it out of the pot without disturbing the root ball. Container-grown plants need no pruning.

CARE AND MAINTENANCE

A plant must have enough water during the first few days after planting if it is to develop fresh roots and survive this critical period of its life. It can only supply itself with water after its roots have grown deep into the soil, so make sure to soak the area around the roots. As the roots generally spread some 30—80 cm (1 ft—2 ft 8 in) deep, the shrubs need ample watering at least three times a year for the water to penetrate to their roots. This is most effectively done by setting a small drain pipe vertically in the ground near each shrub, then filling it with water several times in succession. Newly planted shrubs

11

need at least 10 litres of water per 1 m ($^3/_4$ gal per 1 ft) of the shrub's height at each watering. For single specimens scoop out a shallow bowl-shaped depression in the surface soil to retain water so it cannot run away. Do not water deciduous shrubs from September onwards, then their shoots will become well ripened by late autumn.

During the first few years after planting make sure to remove all weeds before they can flower. Shallow hoeing with a sharp hoe is recommended, though deep-rooted weeds should be forked out roots and all. Later, closely planted mature shrubs will form thick ground cover and suppress weeds. Mulching the soil surface around recently planted shrubs also inhibits weed growth and reduces evaporation of water. Peat, composted pine bark and well rotted garden compost are the best materials for mulching.

In late winter or early spring enrich the soil with a $2^1/_2$ cm (1 in) layer of well rotted garden compost free from weeds. Young and particularly demanding plants can be fed with a solution of compound fertilizer according to the manufacturer's instructions. Divide this amount into two or three doses. Give the first just before growth begins and the last by the end of July at the latest, otherwise the shoots will be late ripening.

Tender species like ceanothus should be given adequate protection before the winter begins. Newly set plants are generally prone to frost damage, particularly young ones whose root system is not yet fully developed. Cover the soil round each shrub with a layer of green brushwood or dry foliage and weight it down with conifer branches, chicken wire or plastic mesh to stop the wind from scattering it. However, most ornamental shrubs that flower in summer and autumn are not damaged by frost even during quite severe winters, though their shoots could be cut to the ground. Provided the base of the main stem remains alive, cut the branches hard back in the spring and the shrub will rapidly make new growth from the roots.

Heavy snowfall damages conifers and evergreens, and thickly-branched deciduous shrubs, so shake the snow off their branches before it causes trouble. In country gardens, ornamental shrubs often suffer from browsing by hares and deer. Protect them where necessary with plastic or wire netting.

PRUNING

Some species such as witch hazels (*Hamamelis*), magnolias, stagshorn sumachs (*Rhus typhina*) and brooms (*Cytisus*) require hardly any pruning and can be allowed to develop their natural shapes. But most species benefit from regular pruning, which consists mainly of removing dead, diseased and damaged branches. Also cut back old, poorly flowering branches to stimulate the growth of vigorous young shoots that will flower profusely. Thin them out every two to four years by

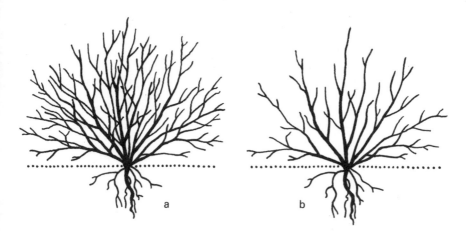

Pruning
before thinning out (a), after thinning out (b).

cutting off the oldest branches just above ground level. If this is not
done in good time, shrubs tend to grow too thick, flower poorly and
soon become old and unsightly.

The time to prune depends on the shrub's flowering season. It is
helpful to group shrubs in two categories:

1) those that flower on the previous year's growth;
2) those that flower on the current season's growth.

Flower initiation takes place as early as the end of the growing season in mid-August on the shrubs of the first group, with flower buds
developing along the shoots. These include witch hazel (*Hamamelis*),
forsythia, lilac (*Syringa*) and viburnum. They are pruned soon after
they have flowered so they can develop strong shoots until autumn.
Shrubs that bear flowers on the lateral branchlets growing from two-
year or older branches need only occasional thinning out, removing
the oldest growth and weakest shoots. This applies to cherries and
laurels (*Prunus*), crab apples (*Malus*), hawthorns (*Crataegus*), barberries (*Berberis*), cotoneaster, pearl bushes (*Exochorda*), flowering
quinces (*Chaenomeles*), laburnum and flowering currants (*Ribes*).

Shrubs in the second group produce their flowers in the year they
have been initiated, which is why they flower later than those of the
first group, in summer and autumn. To ensure a good crop of flowers,
pruning is carried out in late winter or early spring, while the shrubs
are still dormant. They include buddleia, bladder senna (*Colutea*),
rose mallow (*Hibiscus*), hydrangea, St John's wort (*Hypericum*), mock
orange (*Philadelphus*), *Spiraea* × *bumalda*, weigela and other genera
from more favourable climates.

Slow-growing shrubs such as *Acer palmatum*, aralia, mezereon

13

(*Daphne*), beauty bush (*Kolkwitzia*), witch hazel (*Hamamelis*) and *Prunus triloba* are better not pruned at all. Only remove dead or damaged growth. Rapidly growing shrubs, on the other hand, can be pruned every year.

Shrubs that have grown too old or have lost many of their lower leaves can be rejuvenated by pruning, either radically or gradually over two or three seasons. Cut them back to 5—30 cm (2—12 in) from the ground, preferably while they are dormant. Shrubs that are too overgrown or neglected are best replaced with young ones.

Remove all shoots that grow from the rootstock of grafted shrubs during the growing season to prevent the plant becoming exhausted and the rootstock swamping it.

After cutting back a large branch pare the wound clean with a knife and paint it with bitumen paint to exclude disease spores. Take cut branches to the bonfire immediately, as they can become a source of infection and pests. Use proper, good quality tools for pruning — a sharp gardening knife or a pair of secateurs (preferably one with a pair of blades rather than the anvil type) for cutting shoots up to 1$^1/_2$ cm ($^1/_2$ in) thick and a pruning saw for thicker wood.

PROPAGATING ORNAMENTAL SHRUBS

Nurserymen propagate ornamental shrubs sexually (i. e. from seeds) or by various vegetative methods, either direct (cuttings, division or layering) and indirect (grafting and budding). Amateurs can use all these methods. Raising young plants saves you money and gives you pride in your own work.

Propagation from seed

Only species that produce seeds that will germinate in our climatic conditions are propagated this way. It is a cheap method, but rather slow. Another drawback is the probable variation in the offspring, which may not be exact replicas of their parents. This applies particularly to species and cultivars that can be crossed easily. Gather the fruits and seeds when they are ripe, but only use healthy, carefully selected plants for propagation. Do not allow seeds to get overripe or they could fall to the ground before they are gathered. It pays to gather the fruits of some species a little earlier, as the fully ripened seeds contain substances that inhibit rapid germination. This is true of roses, cotoneasters, hawthorns (*Crataegus*), flowering quinces (*Chaenomeles*) and several others.

Gather dry seed receptacles such as capsules, pods and bladders and spread them on a sheet of paper in a warm, dry and well-ventilated place. The seeds will drop out by themselves or can be removed from their pods when dry. Store them in a dry and well-ventilated place until spring. With fleshy fruits, first remove the fleshy covering. They can be gently crushed and the seed separated on a sieve under running water, or they can be left to dry and the seeds later removed.

Some seeds must be prepared for sowing in advance, as they cannot be stored in a dry place for a long time. The drying out delays germination, so that the seeds take two, three or even four years to germinate. To break hard seed coats and speed up germination, soak such seeds in tepid water for anything from several hours to several days according to the species.

Seeds of many species do not germinate unless they are stratified. After harvesting bury such seeds immediately in moist sharp sand or a mixture of peat and sand in a box, pot or other suitable container and keep them slightly above freezing till the following spring. Plunge the container in the garden or store in a cellar or deep frame. Make sure the sand is neither waterlogged nor too dry, or the seeds could turn mouldy or dry out and fail to germinate. Stratified seeds will swell considerably, their hard coats will break and sprouts will appear. This is the time to sow them.

The best time for sowing is February to March. Sow the seeds in a well-prepared garden bed free of weeds. Some seeds can also be sown in trays, bowls, pots and tubs, which can be removed to a more favourable spot if necessary. The containers should be well-washed or disinfected to prevent the spread of fungal infection. Put a layer of drainage material in the bottom of the container, followed by proprietary seed compost. The compost surface should be about 2 cm ($^3/_4$ in) below the rim of the pot to allow for watering.

Sow the seeds in drills, being careful not to sow too thickly. Large seeds can be sown individually, fine seeds can be mixed with sand. Regular watering and weeding are essential for germination to take place. Shade from direct sun in the early stages. Germinating seeds should be covered with glass to ensure constant humidity. Optimum germinating temperature for most species is 15—18 °C (60—65 °F). As soon as the seedlings have three leaflets, prick them out into pots or a garden frame. Transplant them the following spring. Plant them out in rows, spacing the seedlings about 10 cm (4 in) apart. Most are then left for a year or two until they are suitable for planting out in the open.

Division

Some ornamental shrubs develop adventitious buds on their shoots. These can be divided into two or more clumps. Dig up the parent plant and separate it into sections, then grow these on like seedlings or plant them in their permanent sites. This method is used with buddleias, for example.

Propagation by suckers

Many ornamental shrubs spread extensively by means of underground suckers. Older plants in particular produce plentiful suckers, thus weakening the mother plant. Propagated in this way are stagshorn sumachs (*Rhus*), snowberries (*Symphoricarpos*) and lilacs (*Syringa*).

Stooling

Stooling is another quite easy method of propagation, though not often used. Cut the mother plant back close to the ground so that it produces many new shoots. When these are a year old, cover them with a mound of loose, humusy soil in spring to encourage young shoots to develop. Stooling should be completed by late June. Remove the soil in the autumn or the following spring; sever the young plant from the mother plant and transplant it to its permanent site in a garden bed. Put the soil back and let the mother plant grow. Heathers (*Erica*) and flowering currants (*Ribes*) can be increased in this way.

Layering

Layering is one of the easiest means of propagation for amateur gardeners. Bend well-ripened annual shoots down to the ground, slit each halfway through towards the tip and cover the wound with soil containing some well-rotted compost, leaving the tip protruding above the surface. Weight the shoot down with a stone. Detach the layered shoots from the parent plant the following year or even later. Examples: rhododendrons, *Forsythia suspensa*, some cotoneasters and viburnums.

Softwood cuttings

Softwood cuttings are best taken in June and July, preferably from lateral shoots. Cut them early in the morning before they can wilt and insert them immediately after they have been taken. To prepare them, cut them back to about 10 cm (4 in) long with a sharp knife. Cut across the base, close to a bud, leaving it as long as possible. Remove the bottom leaves and to limit evaporation, trim the tip leaves to half their original length. Then plunge the prepared cuttings in a 0.2% solution of potassium permanganate or other fungicide.

Rooting can be speeded up by using hormone rooting powder. Moisten the bottoms of the cuttings and dip them in the powder. Make holes in the compost with a dibber and insert the cuttings carefully, so the powder is not wiped off. Pure sand free of any soil makes

16

the best rooting medium. Alternatively use a mixture of pure fibrous peat, river sand and perlite. The container must be well drained.

Give the softwood cuttings a good watering and stand them in a greenhouse or frame, under plastic sheeting or anywhere else that there is enough light and a suitable temperature. The cuttings root at about 25 °C (77 °F) in high humidity. Cover them with thin plastic sheeting and mist them occasionally. When the cuttings have rooted, they can be ventilated. You can also start giving them weak feeds of compound fertilizer solution. Plant them out in their permanent site in a garden bed in spring. Many shrubs can be increased in this way, including buddleias, caryopteris and fuchsias.

Hardwood cuttings

Most ornamental shrubs can be propagated from hardwood cuttings. Cut off one-year-old shoots in winter and make them into cuttings about 15 cm (6 in) long. Cut the shoots across close beneath the bottom bud, making the cut as long as possible to wound the tissues that multiply rapidly. Make the upper perpendicular cut some 0.5 cm (³/₁₆ in) above the bud so that as little water as possible evaporates from the wounded surface. Store the cuttings until planting time. Tie them in bundles and bury outdoors in moss, moist sand or peat, or in a cellar or a cool room.

Early in spring, hardwood cuttings are inserted in a weed-free garden bed. Set them in rows some 5 cm (2 in) apart, with only the terminal buds showing above the surface. Regular weeding and watering are essential throughout the growing period. In the autumn or the following spring, set the young plants out further apart, then plant them in their permanent sites later.

Root cuttings

Plants from the *Rhus, Aralia* and some other genera are quite easy to propagate from root cuttings. Detach healthy roots from a parent plant in autumn and cut them into cuttings up to 10 cm (4 in) long. Insert the cuttings in a box filled with a mixture of sand and well-sieved soil, then cover with a 1 cm (³/₈ in) layer of the same medium and put them in a greenhouse at 10—15 °C (50—60 °F). When the plants have developed enough roots and shoots, they are planted out, preferably in spring.

Grafting and budding

This method of propagation involves uniting part of a desirable ornamental or fruiting plant (the scion) with another well-rooted plant, termed the rootstock. It is used mainly for cultivars which are difficult to increase by other means. The main difference between grafting and budding is that grafts have several buds, but budding involves joining a single-bud scion to a stock. The specimens grafted together should be of the same species or genus or at least closely related. Choose the scion and stock that will quickly make the growing union.

Winter grafting is carried out in a greenhouse. The rootstocks are grown in containers, with the main trunk preferably not more than 1 cm ($^3/_8$ in) in diameter. Keep the greenhouse temperature at 8—10 °C (42—50 °F), increasing it gradually to 16—19 °C (61—66 °F) in the course of a month. By this time, the stocks will have started to grow and can be grafted. Store the scions in a cool place to prevent precocious growth. The newly grafted plants require a constant temperature of 18 °C (65 °F). After the two parts have grown together and the graft puts out new shoots, lower the temperature to 10—12 °C (50—54 °F) and reduce watering. Pinch the new shoots above the third leaf to produce a well-branched crown. Plant out the grafts in nursery rows from late May onwards. After another two years transplant them to their permanent sites. Spring grafting is also done under glass, while in summer it can be performed out of doors. Only a single bud is left on green grafts.

Budding is usually done in February and March in a greenhouse or in July and August in the open. The buds are reluctant to establish during summer droughts.

SPECIMEN SHRUBS

Specimen plants do not need to be trees or large shrubs. In a small garden, a striking compact shrub grown in isolation can serve the same purpose. Specimen shrubs need enough space to develop naturally and display their attractive features. Give them plenty of sunlight too, planting them in a south or south-west aspect. Most impressive are single specimens growing in a well-maintained lawn, on a bed of low-growing perennials or a rock garden. Where the ground undulates, these shrubs are best sited on the higher ground.

In a garden designed to fit into the natural landscape, a solitary shrub may not be sited in the middle of the garden. It is better to position it where it can be easily seen from a window, a garden arbour or some other place where you spend much of your free time. A solitary shrub planted near a place of rest provides pleasant shade during the midday heat in summer. In a large garden, a specimen shrub could be set near an architectural feature such as steps, pools, house gates, paths or some other place that needs to be highlighted. Never plant tall woody plants in front of windows, but allow the sunlight free access to the house.

For a few years after planting, a specimen shrub may seem too

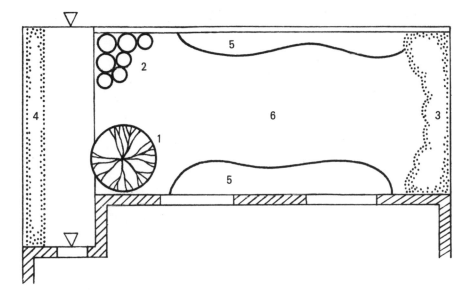

Ornamental shrubs in garden design: 1. specimen shrub 2. groundcover shrubs 3. informal hedge 4. formal hedge 5. annuals and perennials 6. lawn.

small for your garden. But do not be in a hurry to fill the space with other plants or you will have to remove the overgrown specimens in the future. The best solution is probably to decorate the space round the shrub with low-growing annuals or perennials, which can later be removed.

In a large garden there will be space for several specimen shrubs in different settings. Where there is plenty of space you could even try planting a group of shrubs of one species. These will then spread to look like one spreading bush. Grouping like this is particularly effective with lilacs (*Syringa*), rose mallows (*Hibiscus*) and mock oranges (*Philadelphus*) as well as other ornamental shrubs. The group can be set in a lawn or surrounded by a colourful carpet of annuals or perennials.

Trees and tall shrubs play a key role in linking a garden with the surrounding landscape. Select them carefully, so they fit in with the natural vegetation of the neighbourhood and display some attractive features. The Cornelian Cherry (*Cornus mas*), for example, is a common shrub, valued for its tiny yellow flowers which appear in the early spring.

In towns where gardens are set close together it is wise to choose other shrubs with striking flowers or attractively coloured foliage. Other suitable shrubs have pleasantly scented blooms or ornamental

19

berries that stay on the branches long after the leaves have fallen, even until late winter.

The demanding, tender species repay the gardener's care with their own exotic charm. But choose carefully, as some can seem out of place among our native shrubs. The following shrubs are particularly suitable for specimen planting: *Acer palmatum*, bottlebrush buckeye (*Aesculus*), Chinese angelica tree (*Aralia*), Thunberg's barberry (*Berberis*), *Buddleia alternifolia*, Carolina allspice (*Calycanthus*), Judas tree (*Cercis*), fringe tree (*Chionanthus*), Cornelian cherry (*Cornus*), smoke plant (*Cotinus*), *Cotoneaster multiflorus*, English hawthorn (*Crataegus*), broom (*Cytisus*), mezereon (*Daphne*), *Deutzia* × *rosea*, oleaster (*Elaeagnus*), European spindle tree (*Euonymus*), pearl bush (*Exochorda*), *Forsythia* × *intermedia*, dyer's greenweed (*Genista*), snowdrop tree (*Halesia*), Japanese witch hazel (*Hamamelis*), rose mallow (*Hibiscus*), sea buckthorn (*Hippophaë*), Snowhill hydrangea, common holly (*Ilex*), beauty bush (*Kolkwitzia*), common laburnum, *Magnolia kobus*, crab apple (*Malus*), woody peonies, sloe, firethorn (*Pyracantha*), azalea, stagshorn sumach (*Rhus*), rose acacia (*Robinia*), dog rose (*Rosa*), garland spiraea, bladdernut (*Staphylea*), lilac (*Syringa*), tamarisk (*Tamarix*), fragrant viburnum and weigela.

In small gardens, dwarf woody plants can also be planted singly as, for example, shrubby cinquefoils (*Potentilla*) or cotoneasters.

INFORMAL HEDGES

Hedges provide a boundary to the garden, help give it that desirable feeling of intimacy and shelter it from noise, dust and petrol fumes as well as from strong winds. They help create the garden's microclimate too. Impenetrable hedges can prevent uninvited strangers from entering. They are also used to mask unsightly spots or to divide a garden into compartments, making a break between the house and a sunbathing area near a pool, or a children's playground.

Those opposed to hedges claim that they harbour pests. If they do, they also provide nesting places for insect-eating birds. They certainly take nutrients from the soil, but they also enrich it each year with dead foliage which rots down to form humus. Probably the only valid objection to hedges is that they take up more room than fences.

Informal hedges and screens should be at least 2 m (6 ft 7 in) high to do their job properly. Choose fast-growing, well-branching, undemanding, relatively inexpensive species with thick foliage. Attractive flowers, decorative fruits or impressive autumn foliage are also of interest to the gardener. To achieve a well-balanced effect, it would probably be wise to avoid shrubs with striking foliage. You can enjoy a variety of shapes and colours even in quite a small garden. Once the shrubs are carefully selected, the hedge is decorative almost all the year round.

To avoid overcrowding in a screen planting, select only shrubs whose eventual size will be in scale with the garden. When planning a planting scheme, give each shrub generous room, otherwise a sunlit garden could soon become an impenetrable jungle. Of course, the height of a shrub will be influenced to some extent by how it is looked after. Plants grown in poor, dry soil will be smaller than those in deep moist soil. Do not let the lush-growing plants rob the space needed by their weaker neighbours.

To avoid a dull garden, arrange various species in groups of different shapes and heights. Maintain a balanced layout by planting tall shrubs to conceal some parts of the garden together with low-growing ones that will keep the view open. A small tree such as a maple (*Acer*), rowan (*Sorbus*) or Japanese flowering cherry (*Prunus*) makes a good focal point when planted among shrubs. Do consider its ultimate dimensions so that it does not spoil the view from the neighbouring garden or touch the telephone or electric wires. Most shrubs look best planted in generous groups of a single species, using three, five, seven or even more plants per group. Some shrubs can be pushed slightly forward to create a more natural composition. Planting shrubs like this makes an irregular but balanced layout. Graceful lines of loose groupings, with a variety of shapes and colours throughout the year are more natural than regular shapes and geometrically planted groups.

The spacing of shrubs in a group will depend on the situation, climate and soil as well as the height of the species and varies from 0.5 to 1.5 m (1.8 ft—5 ft). Plants set too close together will be weak, lank and easily bent. On the other hand, sparse planting will not make a very elegant layout. The rule of thumb is to plant tall woody plants in the background and medium-sized and low-growing ones in the foreground. But in a small garden where space is limited, one row of shrubs along a fence will do.

Select ornamental shrubs for informal hedges carefully to create a balanced whole. Never plant shrubs or trees with poisonous flowers, fruits, leaves or bark near a children's playground. Examples of these are mezereon (*Daphne*), laburnum, common buckthorn (*Rhamnus*), poppy (*Papaver*), rose acacia (*Robinia*), snowberry (*Symphoricarpos*) and viburnum.

So many plants are suitable for informal hedges that it is only possible to mention the species that appear in the pictorial section of this book: bottlebrush buckeye (*Aesculus*), amorpha, Thunberg's barberry (*Berberis*), butterfly bush (*Buddleia*), Carolina allspice (*Calycanthus*), Siberian pea shrub (*Caragana*), quince hybrids (*Chaenomeles*), white fringe tree (*Chionanthus*), bladder senna (*Colutea*), white dogwood (*Cornus*), common hazel (*Corylus*), smoke bush (*Cotinus*), *Cotoneaster multiflorus*, English hawthorn (*Crataegus*), *Deutzia* × *rosea*, oleaster (*Elaeagnus*), European spindle tree (*Euonymus*), pearl bush (*Exochor-*

da), Forsythia × *intermedia,* witch hazel (*Hamamelis*), rose mallow (*Hibiscus*), sea buckthorn (*Hippophaë*), Snowhill hydrangea, English holly (*Ilex*), kerria, beauty bush (*Kolkwitzia*), common laburnum, privet (*Ligustrum*), Tartar honeysuckle (*Lonicera*), box thorn (*Lycium*), mahonia, crab apple hybrids (*Malus*), mock orange (*Philadelphus*), ninebark (*Physocarpus*), shrubby cinquefoil (*Potentilla*), sloe (*Prunus*), hop tree, firethorn (*Pyracantha*), common buckthorn (*Rhamnus*), rhodothypos, Alpine currant (*Ribes*), dog rose (*Rosa*), common elder (*Sambucus*), sorbaria, garland spiraea, bladdernut, snowberry (*Symphoricarpos*), lilac (*Syringa*), guelder rose (*Viburnum*) and weigela hybrids. As with specimen shrubs, only one species is mentioned, but most species of the genera listed have similar requirements and serve the same purpose.

FORMAL HEDGES

The smaller the garden, the more desirable a formal hedge is, since it takes up less room than an unclipped one. Unfortunately, regular clipping deprives hedging plants of their annual crop of flowers.

Clipped hedges can be divided into three groups according to their function: 1) low — used to edge beds and paths. They are formed of shrubs that can be clipped to about 0.5 m (20 in) high; 2) medium — used to screen the boundaries of a town house, courtyard or front garden. They reach a height of 0.5—1.5 m (20—60 in); 3) tall — used to form impenetrable green barriers in large gardens and parks and growing 2 m (6¹/₂ ft) or more high.

Maintaining formal hedges demands a lot of time, energy and skill, for they must be clipped and fed regularly. When planting a hedge, prepare the soil well and add fertilizer, as regular pruning deprives the shrubs of nutrients that should be regularly replaced. The roots of some ornamental shrubs can penetrate far into neighbouring lawns or flower beds. This can be prevented by plunging a sheet of metal or other suitable barrier some 35 cm (14 in) wide vertically in the ground about 0.5 m (20 in) from the hedge.

When planting a single row of shrubs to make a hedge, space them 20 cm (8 in) for a low hedge, 35 cm (14 in) for a medium one and some 50 cm (20 in) for high hedges. Being narrower and more easily clipped, single row plantings make the best display.

Tall-growing screens can only be made of privet, hornbeam or holly, for other shrubs tend to lose their bottom leaves. This is why it pays to keep a conical shape, wide at the bottom and narrow at the top with a slope of about 5 to 8% from the vertical.

To form a thick hedge with shrubs well-branched from the very bottom, cut their shoots back hard at planting time to reduce their height by a half to two-thirds. Do not let the shoots grow more than 10 cm (4 in) long each year.

Trimming formal hedges.

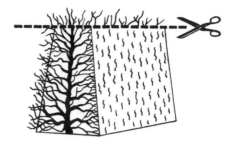

Carry out winter pruning while the plants are dormant, between November and March. Summer pruning is best done in June, after the plants have finished their spring growth. Lush-growing species can be trimmed several times a year. If there are any birds' nests in a hedge, do not clip it till the end of July. In small gardens, hedges are best clipped with shears, but a long hedge is easier to manage with an electric hedge trimmer. Chemical growth inhibitors such as ICI Cutlass slow the growth of new shoots and encourage branching.

Combined fences and hedges can sometimes be seen in the countryside. A fence about 1 m (3¼ ft) high is used to keep game birds or hares out of the garden. Shrubs are then planted about 15 cm (6 in) from the fence so they will rapidly penetrate through the netting and conceal it with their branches.

Unfortunately, only a few ornamental shrubs can bear regular pruning and regenerate rapidly. They include: field maple (*Acer campestre*), Thunberg's barberry (*Berberis*), common box (*Buxus*), pea tree (*Caragana*), hornbeam (*Carpinus*), quince hybrids (*Chaenomeles*), white dogwood (*Cornus*), English hawthorn (*Crataegus*), Forsythia × *intermedia*, rose mallow (*Hibiscus*), English holly (*Ilex*), common privet (*Ligustrum*), mock orange (*Philadelphus*), ninebark (*Physocarpus*), shrubby cinquefoil (*Potentilla*), firethorn (*Pyracantha*), Alpine currant (*Ribes*), snowberry (*Symphoricarpos*) and small-leaved lime (*Tilia*). Other cultivars and species of the same genera are suitable for clipped hedges too.

GROUNDCOVER SHRUBS

Once one could only see areas densely covered with low-growing woody plants in parks, but this practice has become widely used in gardens more recently. Its main virtue is that it forms a thick carpet impenetrable to weeds within a few years. It also succeeds on sloping sites where grass would be difficult to mow.

Best suited for this purpose are ornamental shrubs that grow no more than 50 cm (20 in) high, but spread extensively by means of underground suckers. Examples are St John's wort (*Hypericum*) and periwinkle (*Vinca*). Also suitable are species with arching branches that readily root on touching the ground, such as *Cotoneaster dammeri*. If posible, choose evergreen species whose leaves persist throughout the winter.

Shrubs used for groundcover are low-growing and well-branched with modest soil requirements. As they regenerate quickly, they soon make new growth after being pruned. Many species thrive on sunny sites, others will grow equally well in partial shade under sparse trees or shrubs. When choosing a shrub, always bear in mind whether your soil is acid or alkaline. To bring a larger area to life, plant a taller conical or columnar shrub or tree in a carpet of low-growing shrubs. The smaller the garden, the lower the groundcover should be, of course.

Prepare the soil thoroughly before planting. Remove all persistent weeds, as the shrubs will remain there for decades. Two- to four-year-old container-grown plants are best for planting. Use three to six plants per a square metre (square yard).

Thick and extensive groundcover can be cut with a hover mower. Most species will stand this and form a thick carpet.

Best groundcover shrubs include common box (*Buxus*), quince hybrids (*Chaenomeles*), *Cotoneaster dammeri*, dyer's greenweed (*Genista*), St John's wort (*Hypericum*), privet (*Ligustrum*), mahonia, shrubby cinquefoil (*Potentilla*), firethorn (*Pyracantha*), Spiraea Bumalda hybrids, Chenault's snowberry (*Symphoricarpos*) and *Viburnum carlesii*.

SHRUBS IN CONTAINERS

'Mobile greenery' makes both modern and historic parts of our cities and towns pleasant to look at. Ornamental plants in large containers are commonly used to decorate streets, squares and other public spaces. Once, only profuse-flowering annuals and perennials were used for such decoration, but ornamental shrubs are now encountered too. Containers are usually sited where there is no foliage, on concrete, asphalt and paved areas in busy parts of the town. They serve a similar purpose in gardens, on terraces, large balconies, patios, sun roofs and near arbours.

The size of the container will depend on whether the shrub is to overwinter in the garden or be taken indoors. Containers are made of ceramic materials, reinforced concrete, glass-reinforced plastic or wood. They should have drainage holes at the bottom and be slightly wider at the top to avoid undue root disturbance when replanting. They should be substantial enough not to be turned over by strong winds. A size of 1 × 1 m (3¼ × 3¼ ft) and about 45 cm (18 in) high is most suitable.

24

Cover the bottom of the container with a drainage layer of gravel to about one-fifth its depth. Then put in a filtration sheet, which does not disintegrate easily. Fill the rest with compost of a type that suits what you are planting. The basic mixture consists of fibrous peat, loam, leafmould, sand, perlite and crushed polystyrene flakes. The plants also need a supply of nutrients, preferably 2—3 kg ($4^1/_2$—$6^1/_3$ lb) of compound fertilizer per 1 m^3 (1 cu. yd) of compost. Supplementary feeding is carried out with 0.5% solution of a liquid fertilizer every fortnight throughout the growing season. Before winter comes cover tender plants with brushwood or move them to a frost-free place.

The most suitable shrubs for containers are low-growing species and cultivars such as Thunberg's barberry (*Berberis*), quince hybrids *(Chaenomeles)*, smoke bush (*Cotinus*), *Cotoneaster dammeri*, Warminster broom (*Cytisus praecox*), *Forsythia* × *intermedia*, dyer's greenweed (*Genista*), rose mallow (*Hibiscus*), sea buckthorn (*Hippophaë*), Snowhill hydrangea, St John's wort (*Hypericum*), beauty bush (*Kolkwitzia*), common laburnum, mahonia, crab apple hybrids (*Malus*), shrubby cinquefoil (*Potentilla*), firethorn (*Pyracantha*), azalea, stagshorn sumach (*Rhus*), Alpine currant (*Ribes*), garland spiraea and *Viburnum carlesii*.

The selection could be much wider, provided local climate, container size and the amount of care given to the plants are taken into consideration.

SHRUBS FOR A ROCK GARDEN

Rock gardens have become popular with many gardeners and can be found in many a modern garden. As it is a kind of miniature landscape, it should not be deprived of woody plants, particularly the dwarf and low-growing forms. Unfortunately, deciduous shrubs have not yet become popular with rock gardeners.

The most suitable site for a rock garden is some prominence, perhaps a natural slope, an artificial mound along a drive or a bank beneath a house terrace. An attractive rock garden should display a variety of shapes as well. There should be sheer slopes with montane rock plants, a mountain meadow with exotic species of bulbous and tuberous plants, a heath garden as well as a pool with aquatic and moisture-loving plants. When choosing a shrub for a rock garden, always bear in mind its ultimate size and its soil and climatic requirements. Deciduous shrubs look best planted as solitary specimens, with prostrate perennials forming a suitable undergrowth. Nature teaches a gardener best where to place them. Try to make use of their particular habit of growth, using pendulous or prostrate cotoneasters to conceal a large stone, for example. Ornamental shrubs can

25

link the rockery with the rest of the garden, making it a balanced whole.

Ornamental shrubs generally have no special requirements as regards situation and thrive in almost any garden soil. The only exception are lime-hating shrubs, suitable for heath gardens, which grow best in a mixture of peat, leafmould and sand.

When choosing a shrub for the rockery, consider the type of stone it is built of. A rock garden built of sandstone or granite will suit different species from one built of limestone. The compost can also vary according to the type of stone, the basic ingredient being weedfree topsoil mixed with sand, peat, fine gravel or well-rotted compost.

Do not avoid tender species, even in harsher districts. They will be safe under a layer of dry foliage, peat or green brushwood, provided they are covered before frosts arrive.

The following shrubs do not grow too high, so are suitable for a rock garden: *Acer palmatum*, *Berberis buxifolia*, *Betula nana*, common box (*Buxus*), Japanese quince (*Chaenomeles*), *Cotoneaster adpressus*, *Cotoneaster dammeri*, fishbone cotoneaster, corkscrew hazel (*Corylus*), *Cytisus decumbens*, mezereon (*Daphne*), dyer's greenweed (*Genista*), St John's wort (*Hypericum*), *Paeonia suffruticosa*, shrubby cinquefoil (*Potentilla*), *Prunus triloba*, azalea, Japanese apple rose (*Rosa rugosa*), *Viburnum carlesii* and guelder rose 'Nanum' (*Viburnum*).

Many other species and genera of dwarf deciduous shrubs and conifers are cultivated in rock beds, on dry walls and in troughs or sinks. Besides the species illustrated, the pictorial section of the book also lists many others, which can be grown like this.

COLOUR PLATES

Smooth Japanese Maple
Acer palmatum   Aceraceae

Acer palmatum is a striking shrub, which looks well planted among prostrate perennials in a rock garden, near a garden pool or set in a carpet of heather. Large plants make delightful specimen shrubs in lawns or paved areas. *A. palmatum* can also be potted in a shallow container and trained as a bonsai.

Shrubby maples do best in a humus-rich, slightly acid soil. They dislike direct sun. The variegated cultivars benefit from a slightly drier soil. All varieties are best planted in spring so they have enough time to make new roots before the onset of winter. Keep the rootball intact. No regular pruning is required, only cut back frost-damaged branches in spring. Although older plants are fully hardy in our climate, it is wise to protect the soil above the roots with a thick mulch during the first years after planting. The choice cultivars are more delicate than the species itself.

Shrubby maples are raised from stratified seeds in early April. Cultivars can be propagated from cuttings in March or June, or grafted on *A. palmatum* stocks in late winter.

The Japanese Maple, (*A. japonicum*), is grown in a similar way. A native of the mountain forests of Northern Japan, it grows up to 3 m (9¾ ft) high in our climate. The five- to seven-lobed leaves are 8—14 cm (3¼—5½ in) long and crimson-red in autumn.

A. palmatum is native to Korea, Japan and Northern China, where it grows up to 8 m (25 ft) high in humid situations. In Britain it reaches a maximum height of 2.5 m (8½ ft). The branches are arranged like the spokes of an umbrella (2). In June, they carry clusters of small purple-brown flowers (1). The fruits are

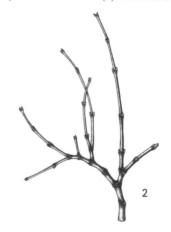

28

reddish two-winged samaras or 'keys', 2—3 cm ($^3/_4$—$1^1/_8$ in) long, each containing a nut with one or two seeds.

The species has fresh green, five- to seven-lobed leaves, which turn crimson-red before they fall (3). The cultivar 'Atropurpureum' has dark red leaves throughout its growing season. 'Aureum' is golden yellow; 'Dissectum Variegatum' bronze-red, tipped pink and cream; 'Dissectum' has narrow-lobed green leaves (4) turning yellow-red in autumn; 'Dissectum Ornatum' is green in summer and red-brown in early spring and autumn.

Bottlebrush Buckeye
Aesculus parviflora

Hippocastanaceae

The Bottlebrush Buckeye is attractive planted as a lone specimen or in small groups. It is also suitable for underplanting deciduous trees with sparse crowns. It is happy in an open, sunny situation, but tolerates light semi-shade beneath taller trees. It thrives in a fairly heavy, well-drained and humus-rich soil. It is fully hardy and tolerates atmospheric pollution.

It is best to plant container-grown seedlings, but bare-rooted shrubs can also be planted. Regular pruning is unnecessary, any that is needed being done in winter. Leave its fallen leaves beneath the shrubs where they will enrich the soil with humus and prevent weed growth.

The Bottlebrush Buckeye is easily propagated from suckers. It can also be propagated by stooling, division and from root cuttings in a greenhouse in winter. When buying a young plant, try to choose one with many new shoots.

The Red Buckeye (*A. pavia*) is another shrubby species of buckeyes suitable for gardens. It is native to North America, where it reaches a height of 3—4 m (10—13 ft). Its leaves are five-lobed, its light red flowers arranged in sparse upright clusters that open in June and July. The cultivars 'Atrosanguinea', with smaller dark red flowers, and the more spreading 'Humilis', with paler flowers, are occasionally grown.

The Bottlebrush Buckeye (1) originally grew in the sandy soils of light North American forests, where it reaches 3 m (10 ft) high. It spreads by many underground shoots to form a rather wide mature shrub. The young grey-brown shoots (2) later turn a reddish colour. The leaves are five- to seven-lobed, up to 20 cm (8 in) long, and are deep green with grey-green undersides. Early spring sprouts are bronze brown; the foliage turns light yellow in autumn.

2

The small, four-part white flowers with purple anthers on striking long stamens appear in July and August (3). They are arranged in upright candle-shaped inflorescences up to 30 cm (1 ft) long.

The obovate spine-free fruits (4) are much smaller than those of horse chestnuts and seldom mature in our climate.

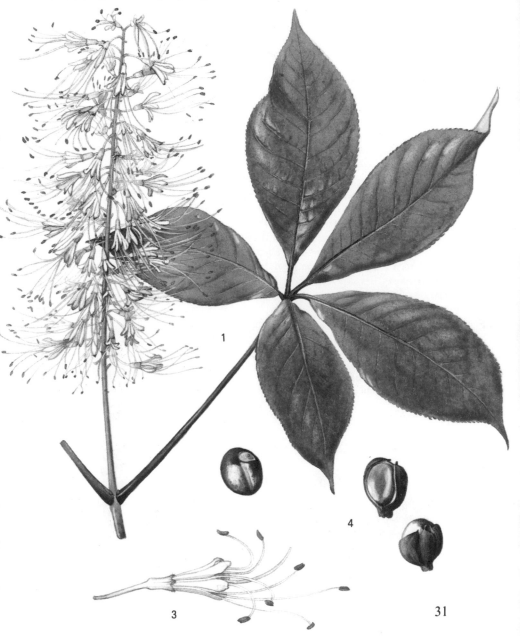

1

4

3

False Indigo
Amorpha fruticosa

Leguminosae

Amorphas are deciduous woody plants particularly suitable for extremely dry sites. They are generally used to anchor soil on sandy hillsides or to form sparse hedges. They can tolerate quite polluted air. Their top growth can sometimes be damaged by frost during a severe winter, but they quickly regenerate, producing plenty of new shoots at ground level. Prune them in spring, because it is the current season's shoots that bear flowers.

Amorphas can be easily raised from seed after the last spring frosts or from hardwood cuttings, which root quite easily when inserted in soil.

A. canescens is a subshrub originally from the arid prairies of central North America. It is excellent for rock gardens and sunny slopes. The spreading, angular branches are covered with grey hairs. The leaves are composed of up to 20 pairs of ovate, felted, greyish leaflets. The spikes of bluish violet flowers are up to 15 cm (6 in) long and open in succession from July to August.

Also native to the North American prairies is *A. nana* (syn. *A. microphylla*), a dwarf species only about 60 cm (2 ft) high. Its shoots (2) are red-brown. The leaves are only 10 cm (4 in) long and formed of 13 to 19 elliptic leaflets with dark spots on the underside. The purple flowers are arranged in short spikes and appear in late June and July.

Amorpha fruticosa originally grew in alluvial soils along North American rivers, but can now also be found growing wild in Europe. It is a sparsely-branched shrub up to 3 m (10 ft) high, forming plenty of suckers. Older specimens frequently lose their leaves at the base and need more frequent rejuvenation, producing new

4

32

shoots even when cut hard back. The
leaves, formed of 11 to 25 elliptic
leaflets, are up to 30 cm (1 ft) long,
slightly scented when rubbed between
the fingers. The type species has
blue-violet flowers arranged in narrow

upright spikes up to 20 cm (8 in) long (1,
3). Flowering time is June and July, but
plants whose frost-damaged branches
were cut back in spring will flower later
in summer. The fruit is a pod containing
1—2 light brown seeds (4). Cultivars
worthy of note are 'Albiflora', with
white and 'Coerulea' with sky-blue
flowers.

33

Hercules' Club, Angelica Tree
Aralia spinosa Araliaceae

Aralias are interesting shrubs making exotic-looking growth. Still rare in gardens, they are more likely to be met in arboreta and botanical gardens, particularly in warm regions. They make spectacular specimen shrubs set in lawns. Though they tolerate partial shade, they flower more abundantly in full sun. They thrive in heavy, well-drained, fertile soils rich in humus. In harsh climatic conditions young shoots should be wrapped with green brushwood before winter arrives. Also protect the soil above the roots with a winter mulch. If branches do get slightly damaged by frost, an aralia will soon produce new shoots in spring.

Gardeners propagate aralias by root suckers or seeds sown in autumn. Sow the seeds in a partially shaded bed. Protect the seedlings with a thick winter covering, especially during the first few years. Variegated cultivars are grafted on to *A. elata* seedling rootstocks in March.

A. chinensis grows wild in Northern and North-eastern China. It is a shrub-like tree, reaching a maximum height of 4 m in European conditions. The bipinnate to tripinnate leaves are up to 80 cm (31¹/₂ in) long, with finely serrated leaflets. The flowers are arranged in oblong-ovate clusters up to 40 cm (16 in) long and appear in August and September.

The Chinese Angelica Tree (*A. elata*), is native to Eastern Siberia, Korea and China. It grows up to 5 m (17 ft) high in European conditions and spreads by underground shoots to form rather ample shrubbery. Its bipinnate leaves are up to 80 cm (31¹/₂ in) long, the leaflets coarsely serrate and prickly on the underside along the veins. The leaves of the cultivar 'Variegata' have irregular white margins.

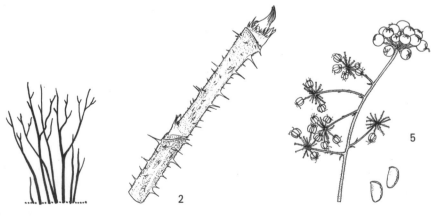

5

2

Aralia spinosa (1) is native to south-eastern parts of North America. It is a rather prickly (2), tree-like shrub growing up to 6 m (20 ft) high. Its bipinnate to tripinnate leaves are up to 60 cm (2 ft) long, the side nerves bend at the edge of the leaf blade. This shrub flowers in July with clusters of tiny five-part, yellow-white flowers (3) arranged in umbrella-shaped panicles (4). The flowers are followed by small black fruits containing 2—5 flat seeds (5).

Thunberg's Barberry
Berberis thunbergii

Berberidaceae

Barberries are among the most popular garden shrubs, thanks to their gorgeous coloured autumn foliage and profusion of fruits. They are equally attractive planted as single specimens or in groups of various sizes. They make good hedging plants, and dwarf forms are most striking in rockeries or planted in tubs and similar containers. Deciduous barberries thrive in a fairly dry garden soil on a sunny site, but do well in any garden soil which is not too thin and poor. They tolerate limy soils and atmospheric pollution. Cut away dead and weak twigs in early spring. Most barberries can be cut hard back.

The type species as well as the red-leaved varieties are raised from stratified seeds in spring. The offspring will vary in character so will need to be carefully selected.

B. aggregata came originally from Western China. It forms a shrub about 1.5 m (5 ft) high. Its light yellow flowers arranged in upright panicles appear in June. The pruinose fruits are salmon-red. *B. × ottawensis* is a hybrid between *B. thunbergii* × *B. vulgaris*, the Common Barberry, and grow up to 2 m (6¹/₂ ft) high with dark red leaves. Its large orange-yellow flowers open in May. *B. × rubrostilla* is only about 1 m (3¹/₄ ft) high. The profuse, pink-red berries are up to 15 mm (⁵/₈ in) long.

Thunberg's Barberry is native to the mountain slopes of the Japanese island of Honshu. It is a well-branched shrub reaching about 1.5 m (5 ft) high. Its angular, red-brown twigs are armed with prickles about 10 mm (³/₈ in) long. The leaves are obovate, up to 3 cm (1¹/₄ in) long and contain the extremely poisonous alkaloid berberine. The autumn foliage is orange-red. The light

3

yellow blossoms (1) open in May, later
producing elongated, glossy red berries
(2) which remain on the branches until
the following spring. Though sour, they
are used to make barberry juice in some
regions.

The cultivar 'Atropurpurea' (3) was
bred in France. It grows about 1.2 m
(4 ft) high, a size that makes it suitable
for low hedges. It is prized for its
red-brown foliage, which will turn a dull
colour when grown in shade, however.
The cultivar 'Atropurpurea Nana' makes
a good rock garden or pot shrub about
30 cm (1 ft) tall.

Dwarf Birch
Betula nana

Betulaceae

Shrubby birches are most suitable for rock and heather gardens. But remember when planting a birch, that its roots are very shallow and spreading, so it robs the surrounding ground of all available moisture. All birches thrive in sunny situations and are fully hardy.

Birches can be planted bare-rooted, but it is better to plant container-grown seedlings, as they can be moved at any time during the growing season. Bare-rooted plants should be planted only in the first few days of budding. No special pruning is required, just remove any dead branches. Do this only in autumn, as in spring fresh wounds exude sap. Birches will not tolerate radical cutting back. The first winter after planting cover the soil over the roots with a layer of leaves, composted pine bark or similar material. Water regularly during the long summer droughts.

Shrubby birches can be propagated from summer cuttings. Specialist nurseries propagate birches by seed in autumn and spring.

B. humilis comes from Central and North-eastern Europe and Asia. It is a shrub about 1.5 m (5 ft) high, occasionally planted in heather gardens and among deciduous shrubs. *B. pumila* is a North American shrub with several trunks, reaching a maximum height of 3 m (10 ft).

Betula nana (1, 2 — buds) is a slow-growing shrub only about 0.5 m (20 in) high. It is widely distributed throughout mountainous parts of Northern and Arctic Europe, Asia and North America, where it usually grows in moist humus-rich peat soils. It is a well-branched shrub that makes creeping growth. Older branches are

2

3 ♀

3 ♂

4

knotty and the bark does not peel off.
Its leaves (4) are only about 15 mm
(⁵/₈ in) long, which is why *B. nana* is
occasionally trained as a bonsai in
a shallow bowl or trough. The female
catkins (3) are stalked, upright and only
7 mm (¹/₄ in) long, while the male ones
(3) are sessile, upright and up to 15 mm
(⁵/₈ in) long. In our climate, flowering
takes place after the leaf-buds have
broken in early May. The upright
'cones' with oval samaras and bare fruit
scales (5) are produced after flowering.

1

5

Buddleia
Buddleia alternifolia

Buddleiaceae

Buddleias are deciduous shrubs frequently grown in parks and gardens. This genus comprises some 100 species chiefly distributed in tropical and subtropical parts of Asia, Africa and America. But only two species are commonly found in our gardens — *B. alternifolia* and *B. davidii* (see p. 42). They are most often planted as specimen shrubs in lawns or beds of low-growing perennials and annuals, as well as among mat-forming woody plants.

Buddleias tolerate almost any garden soil, provided it is not waterlogged. They are fully hardy, so need no winter protection. When buying a new plant, it is best to choose a container-grown one and plant it early in the growing season so it has time to develop new roots before the onset of winter. Young healthy plants do not need pruning, but cut back the old branches of mature shrubs occasionally after flowering to make space for new shoots, which will flower more profusely.

Specialist nurseries propagate buddleias from seed in cold frames as early as January and February. The seedlings are pricked out and later potted in small containers. In the late May they are set in the open ground or plunged in soil in pots. This shrub can also be propagated from softwood or woody cuttings.

The home of *Buddleia alternifolia* (1) is North-eastern China, where it grows to a height of 4 m (13 ft). In European conditions it reaches about 2 m (6½ ft) high. Its long arching branches (2) carry alternately lanceolate leaves about 10 cm (4 in) long and 8 mm (5/16 in) wide, with short stems. The undersides of the leaf-blades are white-felted. This shrub bears clusters of lavender-coloured

flowers along the entire length of previous year's shoots. Each is formed of a four-sepalled, bell-shaped calyx and a four-petalled, trumpet-shaped corolla surrounding four stamens, a style with two stigmas and an ovary with two locules. The flowers' heavy sweet scent may not suit everybody. Buddleias produce much nectar and so are particularly attractive to butterflies. The fruit is a two-valved capsule with remnants of the calyx and corolla.

41

Butterfly Bush
Buddleia davidii

Buddleiaceae

A native of China, the Butterfly Bush can now be found growing wild in many parts of Western Europe. It is most striking whether planted as a specimen shrub or in groups. It is commonly grown near houses, beside roads, where one can closely watch the butterflies attracted to its flowers.

The Butterfly Bush thrives in warm sunny places sheltered from wind. It is best grown in light, well-drained humus-rich soils, preferably slightly acid. Container-grown plants are best planted in spring. Older plants usually do not tolerate replanting. Water liberally during summer droughts. Feed them every 4—6 weeks to keep growth moving, using a solution of compound fertilizer. To maintain the shrub's attractive appearance, cut back the flowered wood. Cut back hard any shoots damaged by frost. They will soon make new growth from the roots. The bark on old branches peels off (3).

The type species can be raised from seed in a greenhouse. Cultivars can also be propagated from softwood cuttings taken from non-flowering shoots. These cuttings root quickly under plastic sheeting in June and July.

Buddleia davidii makes a wide-spreading shrub about 2—3 m (6½—10 ft) high. The young shoots are white and felted, later turning bare. The flowers are borne in panicles about 25 cm (10 in) long, with drooping tips, and appear from June to September. The flowers of the species itself are violet, splashed with yellow-orange at the mouth. They are followed by capsules containing many seeds (2).

The most popular cultivars include: 'Black Knight', with long panicles of dark violet flowers; 'Cardinal', with dark purple-violet flowers in long panicles; 'Empire Blue', with blue-violet flowers arranged in inflorescences up to 30 cm long; 'Fascination', with lilac-pink flowers arranged in panicles about 50 cm (20 in) long; 'Ile de France' (4), with dark violet panicles up to 60 cm (2 ft) long; 'Peace' (3), with 55 cm (22 in)

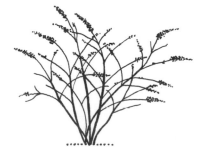

3

42

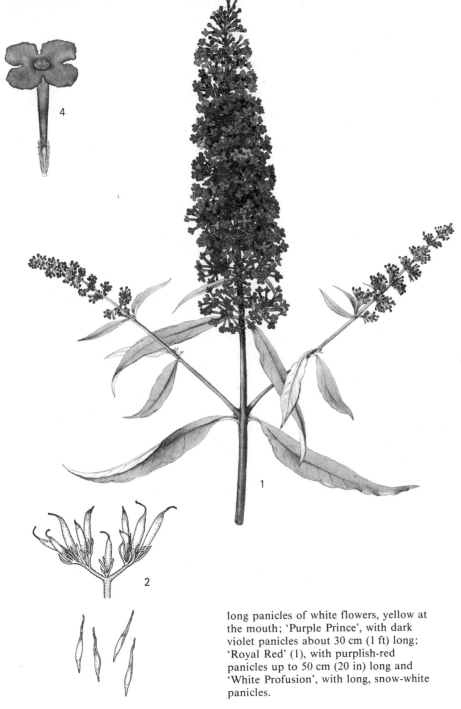

long panicles of white flowers, yellow at the mouth; 'Purple Prince', with dark violet panicles about 30 cm (1 ft) long; 'Royal Red' (1), with purplish-red panicles up to 50 cm (20 in) long and 'White Profusion', with long, snow-white panicles.

43

Common Box
Buxus sempervirens

Some 30 species of box grow in the Mediterranean region, Western Europe, Eastern Asia and Central America. They are shrubs or small trees with evergreen, leathery, opposite leaves. They grow equally well in sun or shade provided the site is not too dry. Their roots tolerate the competition of taller trees.

Common Box used to be a very popular shrub, widely used for topiary and clipped into birds and beasts and geometrical shapes. Nowadays it is more commonly used for low clipped hedges. The plants are long-lived in favourable conditions, but in cool exposed situations they can be damaged by frost every year. The hard wood is a favourite with woodcarvers.

Young plants with balled roots are best planted in spring. Specialist nurseries propagate them from cuttings in August and September. Plants grown from seed vary in their characteristics. Smaller numbers of young plants can be obtained by stooling. Plant a mother plant deeper in the ground than normal or mound it over with soil. When the young shoots have rooted, they can be cut away from the parent shrub and planted in the open ground.

B. microphylla, a native of Japan, is a compact shrub of creeping habit growing no more than 1 m (3¹/₄ ft) high. Its leaves are smaller, only 20 mm (³/₄ in) long. It flowers in April and May and is hardier than Common Box.

The natural range of *Buxus sempervirens* (1) covers the warmer parts of Europe, extending to North Africa and Western Asia. Given favourable climatic conditions, it grows up to 8 m (26 ft) high, forming a shrub or tree with quadrangular, olive-green shoots covered with fine hairs, which usually disappear in maturity. Older wood is protected with shallow-furrowed, black-grey bark. The leaves are about 30 mm (1¹/₄ in) long, yellow-green on the underside. The sweet scent of the small yellow flowers in clustered inflorescences (2) is reminiscent of lilies. They appear in late April and are

3

arranged in clusters in the axils of the leaves. The central female flower is surrounded by several males. The fruit is a leathery capsule (3), with three 'horns', remnants of the styles. Each capsule is divided into three two-chambered valves, each containing two glossy black seeds (4), which mature in October. The most widely cultivated variety is the slow-growing 'Suffruticosa' with smaller leaves. It is particularly suitable for edging flower borders.

45

Carolina Allspice
Calycanthus floridus

Calycanthaceae

Calycanthuses are not spectacular shrubs. In fact, their scent attracts more attention than their appearance. This is why they are usually planted in mixed groups among other more attractive ornamental shrubs. They grow best in humus-rich, well-drained fertile soils and sheltered, sunny or slightly shaded situations. They can tolerate some atmospheric pollution.

They are best planted in spring. Water freely throughout the growing season. Cover them with dry leaves before frosts arrive. Cut back hard any shoots that are damaged by frost in winter. They will be replaced by new growth from the roots. Remove any dead branches when winter is past. No other pruning or cultivation is required, or the shallow, spreading roots could be damaged and the shrub would then produce many suckers.

Calycanthus is usually raised from imported seeds, as its fruits seldom ripen in Britain. You can also try propagating it by layering. This is best done in June, unless the shrub itself produces suckers. Softwood cuttings are very slow to root, even if treated with hormone rooting powder.

C. fertilis (syn. *C. glaucus*) is a slow-growing North American deciduous shrub about 1—2 m high (3¹/₄—6¹/₂ ft). Its faintly fragrant flowers are a lighter shade of red-brown, about 3—4 cm (1—1¹/₂ in) across and appear in June and July. The cultivar 'Nana' is of dwarf habit.

Carolina Allspice (1) is native to south-eastern parts of North America. It grows up to 2 m (6¹/₂ ft) high in our conditions, forming a thickly-branched deciduous shrub with brittle wood. The leaves are up to 12 cm (4³/₄ in) long. When rubbed between the fingers, they give off a pleasant scent reminiscent of strawberries, honey or pineapple. The chocolate brown bark, roots and flowers also contain aromatic essential oils. The olive-brown, bluntly angular, felted shoots (2) have prominent light lenticels.

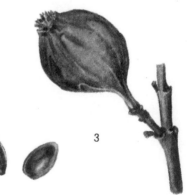

3

46

The single velvety brown flowers, up to 5 cm (2 in) in diameter, open in the axils of the leaves in June and July. The fruits (3) are pear-shaped samaras enclosed in a flask-shaped woody receptable. The brown seeds mature only in warmer regions. Common cultivars are 'Mrs. Henry Type' with larger flowers and 'Purpureus' with reddish leaves.

47

Pea Tree
Caragana arborescens

Leguminosae

Caraganas are excellent shrubs for clipped or untrimmed hedges. They have no special requirements. They are fully hardy in Britain and tolerate dry and sandy soils as well as polluted air. They are happy in partial shade, but flower more profusely in full sun. They are best planted in autumn or early spring. Young bare-rooted plants can be planted, but keep the root balls of older plants intact. No regular pruning is needed, though the plants can be cut hard back if necessary. Young shrubs are sometimes browsed by wild animals.

The type species are propagated from seeds sown directly in an outdoor seedbed, preferably in May. Moisten the seeds with tepid water and leave them for about 12 hours before sowing. Cultivars and small-leaved species are propagated from softwood cuttings under mist propagation. Low-growing species can also be propagated by layering one year-old shoots. Shrubby plants with tree-like trunks are obtained by grafting on to single-shooted rootstock of *C. arborescens* about 1.2 m (4 ft) high. Grafting is best done in early spring in a greenhouse.

C. frutex (syn. *C. frutescens*) is native to Bulgaria and the southern parts of the USSR and grows up to 3 m (10 ft) high. Its yellow flowers open in May.

C. pygmea comes from Mongolia, North-west China and Siberia. It is a shrub only 75 cm (2¹/₂ ft) high, with arching broom-shaped shoots. Its light yellow flowers appear in May.

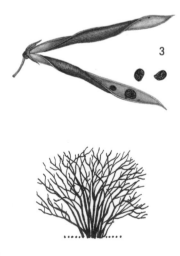

Caragana arborescens is native to Siberia and North-east China, from where it was brought to Europe. It is a sparingly-branched shrub with upright trunks, reaching a height of about 3 m (10 ft). The new grey-green shoots soon loose their leaves. Older branches (2) are dark grey-green and smooth, with large horizontal lenticels. The leaves, formed of about 4—7 pairs of elliptic leaflets, are up to 12 cm (4³/₄ in) long. The light yellow flowers (1) are borne on long stems in clusters of one to three in the axils of the leaves. They appear in May and later produce pods (3) about 5 cm (2 in) long, each with a five-sepalled

calyx at the base. The pods split when
ripe and twist along their axis. The
kidney-shaped seeds mature in July and
August.

The most widely grown cultivars are
'Lobergii' with upright growth and
narrow leaves, and the pendulous
'Pendula', which is grafted on to
a trunk.

Blue Spiraea
Caryopteris × clandonensis Verbenaceae

Blue Spiraeas are very interesting melliferous shrubs and are becoming increasingly popular. In gardens they are usually planted in groups. They make handsome plants for rock or heath gardens as well as for sunny slopes, where they look striking planted among perennials. They grow best in sunny, warm and sheltered sites and light, well-drained and limy soils provided they are not waterlogged.

Before the winter arrives the soil under the shrub should be protected with a layer of foliage, peat or any other material. The tips of the previous year's shoots are usually damaged by frost anyway. Cut them back to about 4 cm of length, preferably in early spring. The young shoots will flower the same year late in summer. Blue Spiraeas are only planted in spring. The root ball must be kept undisturbed. Try to choose the plants which have overwintered without frost damage.

Seedlings are grown from seeds sown in spring, but unfortunately the offspring are rather variable. This is why this shrub is mostly propagated from softwood cuttings taken in June. The cuttings root quite easily under a sheet of glass.

C. incana (syns. *C. mastacanthus, S. tangutica*) is native to Japan, Korea, China and Taiwan. It is an upright shrub about 1 m (3¹/₄ ft) high. Its shoots, young leaves and inflorescences are grey-felted. The violet flowers open from August to October.

Caryopteris commonly grown in gardens are usually hybrids of the species which are more popular than their parents.
C. × *clandonensis* resulted from crossing two species from Eastern Asia, *C. incana* and *C. mongholica*. Its numerous but sparsely-branched shoots grow only about 1 m (3¹/₄ ft) high in our

2

conditions. The leaves are green, grey-felted beneath. Blue Spiraeas flower in the latter half of summer and in autumn. The dense cymes of steel blue-violet flowers (1) with protruding stamens (2) are pleasantly fragrant. The fruits are dehiscent four-chambered capsules.

A highly prized variety is the profuse-growing 'Heavenly Blue' with dark blue flowers.

1

Californian Lilac
Ceanothus hybrids

Rhamnaceae

The Californian Lilac can be planted as a single specimen in grass or in a bed of perennials, but also looks attractive planted in groups of various sizes. Most suitable are warm, dry situations and light, humus-rich soils containing lime. But in semi-shade this shrub will flower poorly. Even though most plants are container-grown nowadays and can be planted out at almost any time during their growing season, spring is still the best time for planting, as it gives the roots time to become established before winter. This shrub needs good drainage, as it cannot bear waterlogged soil in winter. In harsher areas cover the soil over the roots with a layer of peat to ensure safe overwintering. This shrub will still flower, even when cut hard back in spring, as it makes rapid new growth and bears flowers on the current season's shoots. The nut-like fruits (3) are formed of three parts which split apart when ripe.

The species is propagated from stratified seeds, preferably sown in a hotbed. Most cultivars are propagated in summer by layering or cuttings, but some garden forms are better grafted on to *C. americanus* rootstock.

C. americanus grows wild in dry North American forests. It is an upright deciduous shrub about 1 m (3¼ ft) high, with light green young shoots. The leaves are up to 10 cm (4 in) long. The small white flowers arranged in panicles up to 40 cm (16 in) long open on current season's shoots from July to October. The drug prepared from its roots has been used since time immemorial by North American Indians to reduce fever and to heal inflammations of the mucous membranes.

Garden cultivars of *Ceanothus* are more often grown than the species. They are generally called Ceanothus hybrids (1). Most were bred in France at the beginning of this century by crossing *C. americanus, C. coeruleus* and *C. ovatus*. Specialist nurseries offer many cultivars: 'Ceres', lilac-pink; 'Delight', deep blue; 'Gloire de Versailles', deep

3

52

azure-blue with long panicles of flowers;
'Henri Desfosse' (2), violet; 'Marie
Simon', lilac pink; 'Perle Rose',
strawberry pink; 'Topaz', indigo blue;
and many others.

Redbud
Cercis canadensis

Leguminosae

Redbuds can only be grown in warm areas. They look striking planted as single specimens or in small groups. They are happiest in a warm aspect, that is sheltered in full sun and on a limy soil. They will not tolerate waterlogged soils, widely fluctuating temperatures or a polluted atmosphere. Plant them with an intact ball of roots, preferably in spring. The plants may get damaged by frost during severe winters. Cover the surface of the soil round the shrub with a layer of peat or bark chippings before frosts arrive in autumn. Only cut out dead and frost-damaged wood in spring.

Redbuds and Judas Trees (*C. siliquastrum*) are propagated under glass from seeds in spring. Other species and cultivars are best grafted on to *C. siliquastrum* rootstock in a greenhouse in winter. Also try propagating it from cuttings treated with hormone rooting powder. Grow the young plants under glass until they are strong enough to be transplanted.

C. chinensis is a native of China, but has been grown in Japan for centuries. In its homeland it is a tree up to 15 m (50 ft) high. In our conditions it only makes a good-sized shrub. The red-violet flowers open in May, when the shrub is at its loveliest.

C. siliquastrum, the Judas Tree, grows on limy southern slopes from the Mediterranean region to Afghanistan. It is a sparsely-branched tree-like shrub up to 8 m (26 ft) high. In our conditions it only reaches 4 m (13 ft), as it is sometimes damaged by frost during severe winters. The greyish-green leaves (4) are kidney-shaped, cordate at the base and blue-grey on the underside. The shrub bears flowers from April to May before the leaves appear. The purple-pink flowers are solitary or arranged in short clusters. Cultivars worthy of note are 'Alba' with creamy white flowers and 'Bodnant' with rosy-purple flowers.

The Redbud is a North American shrubby tree reaching 12 m (40 ft) in its homeland, but much less in Britain. Old branches become thick and knotty. The deep green, cordate leaves (2) with short apices measure about 12 cm (4$^1/_4$ in) across. They are blue-grey, with sparse hairs on the underside, turning light yellow in autumn before they fall. The clusters of light pink flowers (1) appear before the leaves in April and May and are followed by flat, two-chambered violet-brown pods up to 8 cm (3$^1/_4$ in) long (3). They remain on the tree for a long time. The seeds are flat and smooth. In particularly favourable situations, such as wine-growing regions, redbuds flower a second time in September. Their flowers attract bees.

Flowering Quince, Cydonia
Chaenomeles japonica
(syn. *Cydonia maulei*)

Rosaceae

The genus *Chaenomeles* comprises only four species, originally distributed in Eastern Asia. They are deciduous, rather sparsely-branched shrubs with spiny branches. Their alternate leaves persist into winter. Quinces are planted as individual specimens or in groups and are also suitable for clipped or uncut hedges. Low-growing cultivars are often used to anchor sandy slopes or are planted in rock gardens and in front of taller woody plants. Dwarf quinces stand up to the severest winters and so are popular for groundcover in parks and gardens.

Quinces are quite undemanding woody plants, happy in any normal garden soil rich in lime. They flower more profusely in full sun, though they tolerate some shade. They are best planted in spring or autumn, the low-growing cultivars preferably with the root ball intact. Shoots growing from the rootstocks of grafted plants should be cut hard back to prevent the cultivated variety from turning wild.

The Japanese Quince or 'Japonica' (*C. speciosa*, syn. *C. lagenaria*) is native to China, but nowadays grows wild in many parts of Japan too. It is an upright, much-branched, spiny shrub about 1.5 m (5 ft) high. Its scarlet red flowers up to 4 cm (1½ in) across open in clusters of two to six at the same time as the leaves. As it produces many root suckers, the Japanese Quince makes good groundcover wherever it is needed.

Dwarf Quinces (1) come from the Japanese islands of Honshu and Kyushu. They are spreading shrubs barely 1 m (3¼ ft) high. Their spiny shoots are felted when young, but later become bare (2). They carry broadly ovate leaves about 4 cm (1½ in) long and round stipules. The brick-red flowers about 3 cm (1¼ in) across usually appear in April, shortly before the leaves. They are followed by many-seeded, round, aromatic fruits (3, 4) about 4 cm (1½ in) across, coloured yellowish-green and lightly speckled.

3

They remain on the shrub far into the winter unless eaten by birds. The seeds are brown and drop-shaped. The variety *alpina* is a prostrate shrub growing no more than 40 cm (16 in) high, with fruits about the size of a hazelnut.

Ornamental Quince
Chaenomeles hybrids
(syn. *C.* × *superba*)

Rosaceae

Crossing *C. japonica* with *C. speciosa* has given rise to many Chaeno-meles hybrids (1). The first was produced as long ago as the end of the last century by O. Froebel of Zurich. Cultivars differ in growth habit, size, leaf shape and flower colouring, depending on the charac-teristics inherited from each parent. Unfortunately, some of the love-liest cultivars are not hardy enough in our climate — particularly varieties bred in the more favourable climate of California, U.S.A.

Quinces are raised from seeds in autumn. Sow stratified seeds early in spring. Low-growing branches can be layered, then detached from the parent shrub when rooted. Many cultivars can be propagated from well-ripened cuttings in a propagator in July or August. Treat with hormone rooting powder and maintain high air humidity under plastic sheeting. Cultivars that are difficult to root are better grafted on to seedlings or root cuttings of either species.

The cultivars offered for sale by specialist nurseries include: 'Boule de Feu', salmon-orange; 'Brilliant', large, orange-red flowers; 'Crim-son and Gold', deep red flowers with golden yellow anthers; 'Ernst Finken', scarlet-red; 'Etna', semi-double, scarlet-red; 'Eximia', single, light red; 'Fire Dance', blood red; 'Nivalis', pure white; 'Pink Lady', deep pink and 'Simonii', semi-double, deep scarlet-red flowers.

As quinces flower on the previous years' shoots, the blossoms tend to be hidden among the leaves and barely visible. Only the early-flowering cultivars open their flowers before the leaves, which is why they are so much in demand. The sessile flowers are formed of five petals, with 15 to 50 stamens and five pistils

2

58

1

joined at the base. Besides the
single-flowered cultivars there are also
some semi-doubles. The fruits (2) are
aromatic pomes with five-chambered
cores enclosing drop-shaped brown
seeds. Though rich in vitamin C, quinces
cannot be eaten raw and are only used
to make quince cider and jelly.

Fringe Tree
Chionanthus virginicus

Oleaceae

This interesting shrub, flowering in early summer, has not so far been widely cultivated. It can be planted as a specimen or grouped. It does best in a warm, sunny and sheltered position and deep, loamy soil, which is reasonably moist and rich in nutrients.

Plant the Fringe Tree while it is dormant, preferably in early autumn, so it has time to develop new roots before winter. Container-grown plants can be planted throughout the growing season. Protect the roots with a covering of processed bark or other suitable material during severe winters. Do not plant this shrub too deep, or it will flower poorly.

The Fringe Tree can be raised from seed. Stratify the seeds, as they take a long time to germinate, often two or three years after being sown. In specialist nurseries Fringe Trees are budded or grafted on to *Fraxinus ornus* (Flowering Ash) rootstocks. Grafting is best done in a greenhouse in winter. The grafted plants make more rapid growth and flower earlier in the summer.

C. retusus, the Chinese Fringe Tree, is native to China and Taiwan. It is a shrub about 3 m (10 ft) high, conspicuous by its glossy light brown trunk whose bark peels off in thin layers. The opposite leaves, softly felted on the underside, turn yellow in the autumn. The profuse flowers appear in June and July and are arranged in upright, branched panicles. They are white and fragrant, with narrow petals about 15 mm (⁵/₈ in) long. This shrub is not fully hardy in Britain.

The Fringe Tree is native to North America and grows near streams and lakes, where it reaches tree-like dimensions. In our conditions it forms a spreading shrub about 4—5 m (13—17 ft) high, with olive-green, lightly spotted shoots (2). The leaves are up to 20 cm (8 in) long, turning light yellow before they fall in autumn. It flowers on the previous year's shoots, usually as

early as June. The hanging flower
panicles (1) are about 20 cm (8 in) long.
The four-part, white flowers have
a pleasant scent; the petals are about
25 mm (1 in) long, accrete at the base.
In full blossom this shrub looks as if
covered with snow. The flowers are
followed by single-seeded blue-black
oval drupes (3). Unlike *C. retusus* is is
almost fully hardy in Britain.

Bladder Senna
Colutea arborescens

Leguminosae

Coluteas are planted as single specimens or in mixed groups. Being very adaptable, they are often used as pioneer plants to cover poor soils and unsightly places such as dumps.

They thrive in warm, sunny places. The soil should be light, limy and well-drained. They stand up well to smoky atmosphere. Like other members of the pea family, coluteas can absorb nitrogen from the air by means of the nitrogen-fixing bacteria Rhizobiaceae that live on their roots. When planting a seedling, cut back the tips of the young shoots. Remove any wood damaged by frost in early spring. This shrub will make rapid new growth from the roots. Regular pruning is unnecessary.

Bladder Sennas are propagated from seeds sown straight in a garden seed bed in April. Before sowing them, sprinkle the seeds with warm water so they swell up. Cultivars and delicate species can be grafted on to rootstocks of the type species. Cuttings taken in July root readily under mist propagation.

C. × *media* is a hybrid of *C. arborescens* and *C. orientalis*, with leaves composed of 9 to 13 leaflets. Its orange-yellow flowers open in June and July. The fruit is a pod tinted purplish-red.

C. orientalis (syn. *C. cruenta*) originated in central Asia. The leaves are seven- to nine-lobed, with smaller leaflets than those of the Bladder Senna. The orange-red flowers open in succession from June to September. The fruit is a pod, tinged purplish violet. This shrub needs winter protection.

Bladder Senna comes from Southern Europe and North America. It is an upright shrub about 2—3 m (6½—10 ft) high. The young shoots are grey-green, older branches are grey-black, semi-pendulous, with the bark peeling off in layers. The odd-pinnate leaves are about 15 cm (6 in) long and formed of seven to 13 obovate leaflets. The yellow flowers in few-flowered axillary racemes open in June and July. The fruit (1) is a purplish bladder-like pod up to 8 cm (3¼ in) long, which makes a loud crack when split open. The mature fruits are silvery in colour. They split at the base,

2

but remain on the branches for a long time. Each pod contains 30—40 kidney-shaped dark brown seeds (2), which mature in October.

63

White Dogwood
Cornus alba

Cornaceae

The genus *Cornus* contains some 40 species, growing in the temperate zone of the Northern Hemisphere. The many species of dogwood differ in the environmental conditions they require, so they can be grown in a wide range of situations. White Dogwood looks striking planted in groups and is often used in gardens, parks and landscaped areas.

Most dogwoods do best in full sun, though they tolerate some shade as they originated in thin woodland. They are happy in any garden soil. They tolerate atmospheric pollution and are fully hardy in Britain. No special pest and disease control is required.

Dogwoods can be planted in spring or autumn while leafless. Container-grown plants can be planted at any time of year except in the depths of winter. Species and cultivars with coloured bark need annual thinning and cutting back to stimulate new richly-coloured growth.

The species of dogwoods are increased from seeds sown as soon as harvested. Dry seeds must be stratified for 18 months, then sown in spring. Variegated cultivars are increased from softwood cuttings, White Dogwood also by hardwood cuttings in June. The large-flowered species and cultivars are budded on to *C. amomum* rootstocks in spring. Some dogwoods are propagated by layering young suckers in spring. The rooted suckers are detached the next year and planted out.

White Dogwood (1) is native to Siberia, northern China and Korea, where it forms part of the undergrowth in temperate broad-leaved forests. It is a sparsely-branched shrub about 2—3 m (6¹/₂—10 ft) high with semi-pendulous branches. Its yellow-red shoots are covered with fine bloom when young (2). The opposite leaves about 8 cm (3¹/₄ in) long turn yellow-red in the autumn. The inflorescence is up to 6 cm (2¹/₄ in) across, with yellowish white flowers (3) opening in May and June. The fruits mature in September. They are ovate, white drupes (4) flushed with blue and are about 5 mm (³/₁₆ in) long.

The coloured leaves of the variegated cultivars benefit from direct sunlight.

4

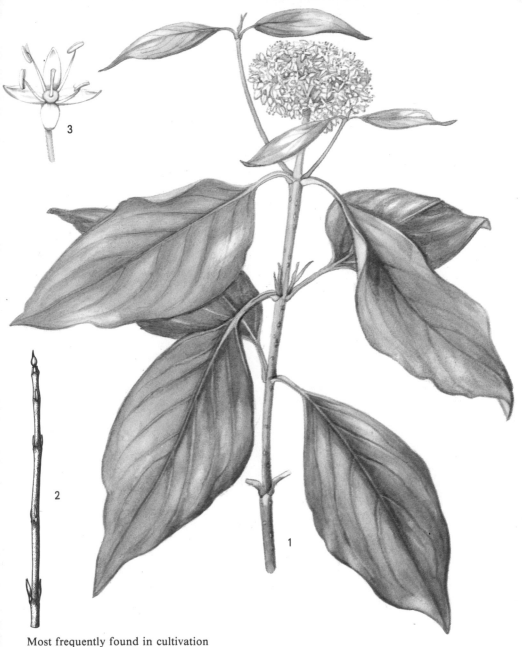

Most frequently found in cultivation are: 'Elegantissima' with wide white margins to the leaves; 'Kesselringii' with brown-green leaves flushed blue and dark purple stems; 'Sibirica' with bright red bark and light green leaves and 'Spaethii' with coral-red bark and the leaves bronze when young, later rimmed with golden yellow.

Cornelian Cherry
Cornus mas

Cornaceae

Cornelian Cherries can be planted as single specimens or in compact groups and are also suitable for clipped hedges. In favourable conditions, they make quite long-lived shrubs.

In North America, the Flowering Dogwood, *C. florida*, grows up to 10 m (33 ft) high, but reaches barely half this height in our conditions. The new shoots are dull red, turning grey-brown as they mature. The oval leaves, up to 14 cm ($5^1/_2$ in) long, turn red-violet in autumn. The small yellow-green flowers are arranged in cymes and supported by four large white bracts. It usually flowers in May. In warmer regions, the ovate, scarlet-red fruits ripen in autumn. This shrub requires a sheltered sunny position and humus-rich soil, which is free from lime. The cultivar 'Rubra' has pinkish red bracts.

C. kousa grows in the mountain forests of Japan, Korea and Central China, where it grows up to 7 m (23 ft) high. Its elliptic tapering leaves are up to 9 cm ($3^1/_2$ in) long. They turn scarlet-red in autumn. The small yellow flowers are surrounded by four yellow-white bracts with curled margins and open in June.

C. macrophylla (syn. *C. brachypoda*), is native to the mountain forests of the Himalayas, China and Japan, where it reaches about 7 m (23 ft) high. The shoots are yellow-brown, turning dark grey when mature. They carry elliptic leaves pointed at the tip measuring about 13 cm (5 in) long and coloured yellow-red in autumn. In our conditions the small yellow-white flowers open as late as July and August.

The Cornelian Cherry is distributed from Southern Europe and Turkey to the Caucasus. It is a wide-spreading shrub-like tree up to 5 m (17 ft) high. The angular young shoots (2) are tinted violet. The bark of older branches is grey-white, peeling off in thin flakes. The ovate to lanceolate leaves up to 10 cm (4 in) long turn yellow in autumn. This shrub flowers on the previous year's shoots as early as March and April, long before its leaves appear. The tiny, four-part golden yellow flowers (1) arranged in umbels are surrounded by an involucre of four bracts. The fruits, borne in September, are elongated, ovate drupes (3) about 15 mm ($^5/_8$ in) long. The yellow-red pulp has a sweet-sour taste. The berries are rich in vitamin C and are used to make preserves, wine and juice. Cornelian Cherries have recently been bred by fruit growers.

Red Dogwood
Cornus sanguinea

Cornaceae

Red Dogwood is a spreading shrub about 4 m (13 ft) high. Producing underground suckers, it is used to anchor crumbling slopes and hillsides. It grows equally well in full sun or shade, in moist or dry soil and is fully hardy in Britain. Its reddish wood is quite hard and heavy and used chiefly for turning and carving.

C. nuttallii is native to the west coast of North America. There it reaches a height of 12 m (40 ft), but grows only about 4 m (13 ft) high in our conditions. The ovate leaves with short, pointed tips are up to 12 cm (4³/₄ in) long. The small yellow-white flowers are arranged in hemispherical clusters and are surrounded by six yellowish white bracts, which are coloured light pink when the shrub is in full blossom in May. The fruits are orange-red drupes.

C. stolonifera is native to the east coast of North America. It is a shrub only 2 m (6¹/₂ ft) high, spreading by numerous underground stems. The new shoots are purple red, later turning darker. The ovate silvery-felted leaves are up to 15 cm (6 in) long and taper at the apex. The small, yellow-white flowers arranged in umbels up to 5 cm (2 in) across appear in May and June. The fruits are almost perfectly round white drupes.

C. alternifolia, a native of eastern parts of North America, is a shrub up to 6 m (20 ft) high with loose horizontal branches. The glossy new shoots are purple-brown; older branches turn black-brown. The leaves are alternate, elongated to ovate, up to 12 cm (4³/₄ in) long and coloured dark violet in autumn. White flowers in umbels about 8 cm (3¹/₄ in) across appear in May and are followed by dark blue fruits on red stems.

Red Dogwood (1) forms part of the undergrowth in the deciduous forests of Western, Southern and Eastern Europe, extending to the Caucasus and Siberia. Shoots growing in shade are

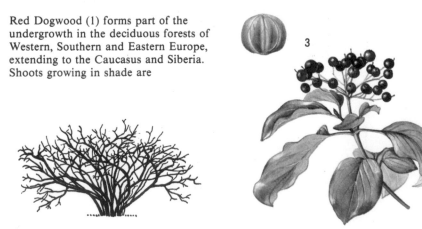

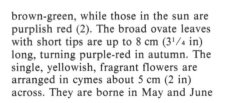

brown-green, while those in the sun are purplish red (2). The broad ovate leaves with short tips are up to 8 cm (3¹/₄ in) long, turning purple-red in autumn. The single, yellowish, fragrant flowers are arranged in cymes about 5 cm (2 in) across. They are borne in May and June and later produce globular blue-black fruits (3) spotted with white on violet-red stems. They mature in September.

Common Hazel
Corylus avellana

Betulaceae

These undemanding shrubs are generally grown in an out-of-the-way corner of the garden. In landscape work they are planted beneath taller trees at forest borders. Common Hazels tolerate full sunlight as well as partial shade and stand up well to smoke-polluted air.

They should be planted while dormant, in spring or autumn. Remove only branches that are causing overcrowding. Specialist nurseries raise the species from stratified seeds (nuts) in early spring, but they can also be propagated by stooling and layering. Cultivars are grafted on to potted rootstocks of the species in greenhouses.

The Purple Cobnut or Filbert, (*C. maxima*), is a tree-like shrub from south-eastern Europe and Turkey. It bears oval leaves and long catkins. The ovate nuts are enclosed in trumpet-shaped husks with toothed margins. Many cultivars have been bred for their nuts, but 'Purpurea' is grown for its ornamental qualities. It has red-black leaves and wine-red catkins.

Common Hazel grows on the edges of woodland and hillsides throughout Europe and Western Asia. It is a rather thickly-branched spreading shrub up to 5 m (17 ft) high. The young shoots are felted, with prominent brownish lenticels. The grey-brown bark on old branches peels off in long layers. The leaves (3) are up to 12 cm (4³/₄ in) long. The pendulous catkins about 5—7 cm (2—2³/₄ in) long, composed of male flowers (1), are formed in the autumn. Female flowers (2) overwinter in buds with the crimson styles protruding, then flower in March. The oval hard-shelled nuts are up to 15 mm (⁵/₈ in) long, each containing one seed enclosed in a green involucre.

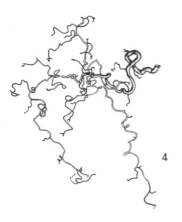

4

The cultivar 'Aurea' is a rather low shrub with orange-yellow shoots. The newly-sprouted leaves are golden yellow, later turning green-yellow with bronze centres. The cultivar 'Contorta' (4), the Corkscrew Hazel, has leaves up to 8 cm (3^1/$_4$ in) long with wavy margins and curiously coiled and twisted branches. They are cut and put in vases for home decoration in winter. 'Atropurpurea' has red-brown leaves. 'Pendula' has a weeping habit and is grafted on to rootstocks of the species.

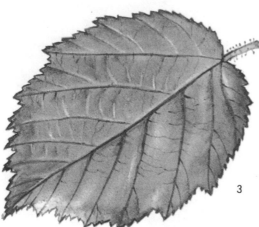

3

Smoke Bush, Venetian Sumach or Wig Tree
Cotinus coggygria
(syn. *Rhus cotinus*)

Anacardiaceae

In small gardens, Smoke Bushes are planted as solitary specimens of exotic growth habit. In large gardens and parks they look well planted in groups or combined with other woody plants. They are happy in fairly light dry soil rich in lime and nutrients. Though they tolerate light shade, they grow best in a sunny position, as direct sun stimulates flower production and a richer coloration of the leaves and fruits. After a severe winter, cut back any weak branches damaged by frost and the shrub will quickly make new growth from the roots. It pays to cover the soil round the shrub with a layer of straw or bark in harsher climates during the first few winters after planting out. Prevent the shrub from becoming too leggy by occasional thinning out, as it can soon reach a diameter of several metres (yards).

The species itself is raised from stratified seeds sown in early spring. You can also try propagating it from root cuttings potted in the autumn and kept in a greenhouse for the winter. When planted out in spring they root quite quickly and start to sprout new leaves. Layering is another way of propagating it, but the shoots must be well rooted, before they are detached from the mother plant, which takes at least two years. Some gardeners succeed in propagating cotinus from softwood cuttings taken in June.

The Smoke Bush (1) is native to an area extending from Southern Europe and Turkey to southern parts of the USSR and Central China. It is about 3 m (10 ft) high and rather wide, as it makes plenty of underground suckers. Its olive brown shoots later turn grey-brown, revealing yellow wood with a strong-smelling sap. The alternate,

4

obovate, deciduous leaves are up to
8 cm (3¹/₄ in) long. They give off
a pleasant scent when rubbed between
the fingers and turn orange-red in
autumn before they fall. The small,
five-part, yellow-green flowers (2) are
arranged in thickly-branched upright
panicles and open in June and July. The
fruits (3) are long-stalked brownish
drupes covered with long reddish hairs
which help the wind carry them some

distance to disperse the fruits when they
ripen.
   Good garden forms are: 'Purpureus'
with purple leaves and hairs; 'Royal
Purple' (4) with red leaves with
a metallic sheen and purplish-pink
hairs; 'Rubrifolius' with dark red leaves
turning greenish in summer.

73

Cotoneaster
Cotoneaster adpressus   Rosaceae

The genus *Cotoneaster* comprises some 50 species, mostly from the Himalayas, Tibet and Western China. Their flowers are inconspicuous but they are valued for their striking ornamental fruits. The upright growing species make attractive specimen shrubs suitable even for small gardens. They are also planted to make unclipped screens and hedges. Creeping cotoneasters make excellent groundcover, while the dwarf forms can be planted against dry walls or in a rock garden.

Cotoneasters have no special soil requirements, being happy even in poor, stony and limy soils on rocky slopes and in exposed positions. Though most species tolerate semi-shade, they produce more flowers and fruits when planted in full sun. The evergreen species are more demanding and require sheltered situations.

Deciduous cotoneasters can be planted bare-rooted, but the root balls of evergreen species must be kept intact. All species are fully hardy, though some evergreens can lose most of their leaves in a severe black frost. Do not prune hard back as new shoots are very shy to sprout from the dormant buds at the very bottom of the shrub. Cut out some of the older branches regularly to prevent them growing out of place and to maintain the desired size and shape.

The species are raised from seeds sown immediately after harvesting. Stratified seeds are sown the following spring. Some garden forms are propagated by layering, deciduous species by softwood cuttings taken in June and evergreens by ripe cuttings in late August.

Cotoneaster adpressus (1) is native to Western China. It is a deciduous shrub of creeping habit, reaching a height of about 25 cm (10 in). Its fan-like reddish shoots (2) spread in all directions. The broadly ovate leaves are up to 15 mm (⁵/₈ in) long and turn red before they

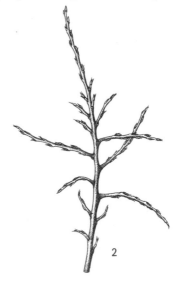

2

fall. The reddish flowers appear in June, followed by light red, globular fruits containing two seeds or nutlets (3). They mature in September. This species is excellent for rock gardens and rocky slopes and can be used for decorating graves.

The most widely grown garden form, 'Little Gem', is a hybrid between *C. adpressus* and *C. horizontalis*. It is a slow grower, forming dense cushions. It bears no fruits and is smaller than the species.

3

1

Cotoneaster dammeri Rosaceae

Cotoneaster dammeri is a creeping shrub about 20 cm (8 in) high with long, arching branches. Its branches root readily where they touch the ground. This is why this shrub is used to cover large areas of bare soil. It makes compact groundcover quite quickly, reducing weeds by carpeting spaces they would otherwise occupy.

The related *C. bullatus*, a native of China, is about 2—3 m (6¹/₂—10 ft) high. The deciduous, lanceolate-ovate leaves are about 8 cm (3¹/₄ in) long. It flowers in May and June with reddish blossoms carried in umbels, followed by globular red fruits. It is among the hardiest cotoneasters.

C. congestus is native to Nepal and the eastern Himalayas. It is a creeping shrub about 40 cm (16 in) high. Its evergreen obovate leaves are almost 13 mm (¹/₂ in) long. The wide-open, light pink flowers are borne in June, followed by light red globular fruits.

C. conspicuus, which came from South-eastern Tibet, is a mat-forming shrub about 1 m (3¹/₄ ft) high. Its elliptic leaves up to 2 cm (³/₄ in) long are covered with thick hairs on the underside. The white flowers open in late May and June and are followed by light orange fruits. This species is best grown in a warm sheltered position. The creeping cultivar 'Decorus' is smaller with dense foliage and a profusion of flowers.

C. dielsianus came from central and western China. It is a wide-spreading shrub with arching branches and grows up to 2 m (6¹/₂ ft) high. Its oval pointed leaves are up to 3 cm (1¹/₄ in) long, grey-yellow felted on the reverse, turning brown-red before they fall. The small pink flowers appear in profusion in June. The fruits are a glossy red.

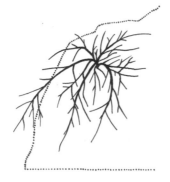

Cotoneaster dammeri (1) is an evergreen shrub from Central China. Its lanceolate-ovate, leathery leaves are up to 3 cm (1¹/₄ in) long. The white flowers suffused with red are carried on short stalks and open in May. The fruits (2) are globular and scarlet-red, containing five seeds and remain on the shrub far into the winter. The variety *radicans* spreads quickly to form a thick groundcover. It is suitable also for harsher climatic conditions. The most commonly grown is the cultivar 'Skogholm'. It is a hardy shrub about 60 cm (2 ft) high, excellent as foliage groundcover for large areas.

1   2

Fishbone Cotoneaster
Cotoneaster horizontalis   Rosaceae

Cotoneaster horizontalis is a creeping or horizontally spreading shrub. It is a delightful plant for rock gardens, as its regular texture makes a striking contrast with lighter stones. It makes a good pot-grown shrub.

    C. divaricatus grows wild in central and western China. It is an upright shrub about 2 m (6½ ft) high. The arching branches carry broadly elliptic leaves up to 25 mm (10 in) long. Its autumn foliage is scarlet-red. Its white flowers open in June, the fruits are coral-red.

    C. franchetii, a native of south-western China, is an evergreen shrub with arching branches, reaching a maximum height of 1.5 m (5 ft). The pointed, elliptic leaves are felted yellowish-white beneath. Each inflorescence is formed of up to 15 pale pink flowers which open in June. The elongated orange-red fruits remain on the branches until October.

    C. microphyllus grows widely in the Himalayas and south-western China. It is a prostrate, thickly-branched shrub up to 60 cm (2 ft) high. The obovate leaves up to 8 mm (5/16 in) long are covered with grey-white hairs on the underside. The white flowers are borne in May and followed by red fruits. It needs a warm, sheltered site.

    C. moupinensis comes from the Chinese province of Szechwan, where it grows up to 5 m (17 ft) high. The ovate leaves with pointed tips are about 8 cm (3¼ in) long. In autumn they turn dark brown with scarlet spots. The many-flowered umbels of pinkish-white flowers open as early as May and are followed by a profusion of red fruits.

The Fishbone Cotoneaster (1), a native of Western China, is a shrub about 60 cm (2 ft) high whose branchlets (2) are arranged in a characteristic herringbone pattern. The leathery leaves with a finely spiny apex are about 12 mm (7/16 in) long. The sessile, blush-white flowers open in June, followed by globular, scarlet-red

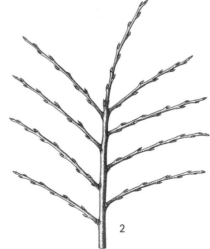

2

fruits (3) about the size of a pea, each containing three seeds (4). The more robust cultivar 'Robusta' has bigger fruits and red-coloured autumn foliage and is hardier than the species. 'Saxatilis' grows much more slowly with shorter branchlets but more flowers and fruits. 'Variegata' is a slower grower than the species with wavy margined leaves spotted with white.

4

1

3

79

Cotoneaster multiflorus makes a good specimen shrub for a small garden. In large gardens and parks it is commonly grouped or planted to form informal hedges.

C. *praecox* is a rather wide but only 50 cm high shrub, originating in Western China. Its prostrate branches easily root where they touch the ground. The elliptic leaves are up to 20 mm (³/₄ in) long, with the underside smooth and lighter in colour. They turn red before they fall. The deep pink flowers are borne on short stalks in May and June. The globular red fruits are up to 12 mm (¹/₂ in) long.

C. *salicifolius* came from western China. It is a shrub with arching branches, which reaches a height of 4 m (13 ft). Its elongated leaves are up to 7 cm (2³/₄ in) long and white-felted beneath. They remain on the shrub until the following spring, when young leaves begin to appear. The white flowers open in June, followed by coral-red fruits. The cultivar 'Gnom' makes prostrate growth. The leaves with blunt bases and apices are up to 2 cm (³/₄ in) long. 'Parkteppich' is a thickly-branched shrub about 60 cm (2 ft) high with larger leaves than the species. It makes good groundcover for large areas.

C. Watereri hybrids (syn. C. × *watereri)*, are mostly hybrids between C. *frigidus* and C. *henryanus, C. rugosus* and C. *salicifolius.* Almost all are evergreen. The most widely grown cultivars are 'Aldenhamensis', 'Cornubia', 'Exburiensis', 'Pendulus' and 'Watereri'.

Cotoneaster multiflorus is distributed from the Caucasus to Western China. It is a spreading shrub about 3 m (10 ft) high, with arching, brown branches. The ovate-elliptic leaves up to 5 cm (2 in)

2

3

long turn yellow in autumn. The umbels of up to 20 flowers open in May. The scent of the white flowers (3) may not appeal to everybody. The scarlet-red fruits (1), about the size of a pea, are borne in profusion at the end of summer. These fruits contain 2—5 flattened seeds with a shiny coat (2). The variety *calocarpus* has larger, more numerous leaves and flowers more profusely than the species. In late summer, its arching branches are decorated with masses of red fruits.

1

Hawthorn
Crataegus oxyacantha

Rosaceae

Hawthorns are among the most popular ornamentals, partly because they make excellent melliferous plants. They are planted as specimen trees or in groups and also make attractive, impenetrable hedges. They are modest in their demands as to soil and siting, growing in any sufficiently deep garden soil, preferably overlying limestone. They tolerate slightly shady places, but do not flower so profusely as in full sun. They can be pruned hard back. Many useful birds make their nests in the tangle of spiny hawthorn branches. Unfortunately hawthorns are hosts of various pests and contagious diseases that affect fruit trees. Hawthorn species are propagated from stratified seeds in spring. The cultivars are budded on to *C. monogyna* seedlings in summer.

The Cockspur Hawthorn (*C. crus-galli*), is native to North America. It is a large shrub with a wide-spreading crown, growing to a height of about 7 m (23 ft). The conspicuous spines are about 7 cm (2³/₄ in) long, the leaves ovate, leathery, up to 8 cm (3¹/₄ in) long. The autumn foliage is orange-red and followed by brown-red fruits.

The Common White Hawthorn (*C. monogyna*), is native to Europe, but occurs widely in North America and Western Asia as well. It is a tree or shrub, often up to 10 m (33 ft) high. Its leaves are three- to seven-lobed, and turn golden-yellow in autumn. The white flowers, borne in May and June, are arranged in small corymbs and have a slightly unpleasant smell. The fruits are dark red and contain a single seed.

Crataegus oxyacantha (1) grows wild throughout Europe and North America, forming part of undergrowth in thin woodland. It is a tree-like shrub with spiny twigs, reaching a height of about 4 m (13 ft). Its three- to five-lobed leaves are shallowly cleft and turn yellow in autumn. Its white flowers open as early

4

as the end of May. The flower corymbs
are composed of 8—12 flowers
measuring about 14 mm ($^9/_{16}$ in) long
and have a pungent smell. The
barrel-shaped, red fruits, which mature
in early autumn, are up to 10 mm
($^3/_8$ in) long (2), each contains
2—3 trihedral seeds (3).

The most widely grown cultivar is
'Paulii' ('Paul's Scarlet') (4), popular for
its double, carmine-red flowers,
arranged in large inflorescences. Less
frequently grown are the cultivars
'Plena' with double, white flowers,
'Punicea' with single, cherry-red flowers
with white centres, and 'Rosea' with
single, pink flowers.

Warminster Broom
Cytisus × praecox   Leguminosae

Some 60 species of *Cytisus* grow chiefly in the Mediterranean region and Central Europe, some also being distributed in Eastern Asia. Warminster Brooms can be planted in heath gardens along with heaths, heathers, junipers and birches. The low-growing species and cultivars make delightful shrubs for rock gardens and good ground-cover too.

Cytisuses need a sunny site and a fairly dry, warm, well-drained soil without lime. They flower poorly in the shade. Species that originated in Mediterranean lands are not hardy in our conditions. Plant them out with a good ball of roots in spring and protect against air frosts with fine plastic netting or sheeting. Cut back long shoots on the tall species, but the low-growing species are better not pruned.

The species are raised from seeds sown straight in pots. Soak them in tepid water so they swell up better. The cultivars are propagated by layering and grafting on to *C. scoparius* and *C. nigricans* rootstocks.

Cytisus × praecox was produced by crossing *C. multiflorus* with *C. purgans*. It is a semi-hardy shrub, which stands up well to polluted air. It makes a lovely specimen shrub, which looks particularly attractive on a lawn or in a large rock garden as well as planted in groups.

C. decumbens grows on limy hillsides in southern France, Italy and Albania. It is a 15 cm (6 in) high, prostrate shrub with five-angled, finely felted branchlets and sessile leaflets about 15 mm (⅝ in) long. Its yellow flowers are borne in profusion from May to June, followed by seed pods covered with fine hairs.

Warminster Broom grows to a height of
1.5 m (5 ft). Its simple leaves with fine
hairs up to 2 cm (³/₄ in) long are borne
on arching branches from mid-April, the
branchlets are completely covered with
creamy white flowers (1, 3). Their scent
may not appeal to everybody. The fruits
are elongated pods (2) with two valves
containing two or more seeds. Several
reasonably hardy cultivars have been
bred in the Netherlands. Worthy of note
are: 'Allgold' with pure yellow flowers;
'Hollandia' with smaller, purple-red
flowers and creamy white-rimmed keels
and 'Zeelandia' with lavish creamy
white flowers with purplish pink wings
and standards.

Common Broom
Cytisus scoparius
(syn. *Sarothamnus scoparius*)

Leguminosae

Brooms have a widespreading root system, penetrating deep into the soil. The roots bear many nodules containing nitrogen-fixing bacteria. They are the plant's greatest benefit, as they enable it to assimilate nitrogen directly from the air. This is why brooms make excellent pioneering woody plants that rapidly cover barren, exhausted soils, that are being restored.

A native of Central and Southern Europe, the Common Broom is found in colonies on grassy hillsides, growing even in dry, sandy and acid soils. The most famous garden forms of broom came from France and later from Great Britain. They were bred by hybridizing the species. Unfortunately, they overwinter safely only in warm regions.

C. × *kewensis* is a hybrid between *C. ardoini* and *C. multiflorus*, growing only 40 cm (16 in) high. Its arching branches carry masses of creamy yellow flowers in May. *C. nigricans* is an upright shrub about 1.5 m (5 ft) high, which originated in central and south-eastern Europe. Its clusters of yellow flowers up to 20 cm (8 in) long open in June and July. *C. purpureus* is native to southern Europe and the Balkans. It is a hardy shrub about 60 cm (2 ft) high. Its purple-red flowers open rather late in June and July.

The Common Broom (1) is a deciduous shrub up to 2 m (6¹/₂ ft) high. Its angular shoots (2) have a typical broom-like appearance. The trifoliate leaves up to 15 cm (6 in) long, are formed of obovate leaflets felted on the underside. The golden-yellow flowers are borne singly or in pairs in the axils of the leaves. They measure about 25 mm (1 in). The fruits are flat, black-brown pods (3) about 7 cm (2³/₄ in) long, containing up to 10 yellow seeds. They ripen in late summer.

The following garden forms are most commonly cultivated in specialist

3

nurseries: 'Andreanus' with yellow
flowers and purple-red wings;
'Burkwoodii' (4) with carmine-red
flowers and brown-red wings rimmed
with golden yellow; 'Daisy Hill' with
pure yellow flowers and red,
white-rimmed wings; 'Dorothy Walpole'
with velvety-red flowers with brown-red
wings; 'Dragonfly' with deep yellow
flowers with brown wings; 'Firefly' with
bright red flowers with yellow wings;
'Fulgens' with orange-yellow flowers
with brown wings; 'Golden Sunlight'
with yellow flowers and 'Killiney Red'
with red flowers.

Mezereon
Daphne mezereum

Thymelaeaceae

Mezereons are most frequently seen planted singly in rock or heath gardens or in grass. They are also used in underplantings beneath taller woody plants. They are happy in partial shade and humus-rich well-drained soils, preferably containing lime. They do not tolerate overfertilized or waterlogged soils. Do not attempt to transplant plants growing in the wild, as they are almost bound to die in your garden. Container-grown specimens bought in nurseries can be planted any time, even throughout the growing season. Mezereons are raised from seeds harvested as soon as the fruits start turning red. The seeds can also be stratified, then sown the following spring. Seedlings are rather variable in growth habit and flower colour, however, so cultivars are propagated exclusively by half-ripe cuttings in early summer. Creeping species can also be increased by layering.

D. cneorum, the Garland Flower, grows in broad-leaved forests and on sunny slopes in central and southern Europe. It is an evergreen shrub about 30 cm (1 ft) high, forming dense masses in the wild. In May it is covered with clusters of fragrant carmine-red flowers. The cultivar 'Eximia' has a more intense colour than the type species.

D. × burkwoodii is a cross between *D. caucasica* and *D. cneorum*. It is a lush-growing shrub about 1 m (3¹/₄ ft) high, with narrow, deciduous leaves. In May its branchlets are hidden under a mass of fragrant, pale pink flowers. The cultivar 'Somerset' has a more robust habit and bears a profusion of dark pink flowers.

Daphne mezereum (1, 5) is scattered through most of Europe, Turkey, the Caucasus and Siberia, where it grows mostly in thin woodland. It is an upright, sparsely-branched shrub, about 1.2 m (4 ft) high. Its lanceolate leaves are about 8 cm (3¹/₄ in) long. The flowers appear before the leaves, as early as March in lowlands and as soon as the snow melts at higher altitudes. Its pinkish-red flowers are very fragrant. The fruits are oval to spherical, scarlet-red (3) and about 8 mm (⁵/₁₆ in) in diameter, with a single glossy brown-black kernel (4). Plants with salmon-pink, scarlet-red and white (2) flowers are also cultivated.

CAUTION: All parts of this plant are extremely poisonous. A few fruits are enough to kill a child. They are eaten by birds, however, which disperse the seeds roundabout.

89

Deutzia
Deutzia × rosea   Saxifragaceae

The genus *Deutzia* includes some 50 species, most of them growing in eastern Asia, except for two species from Central America. Deutzias are upright, deciduous shrubs usually planted singly or in mixed groups. They also make attractive untrimmed hedges. They grow well in any normal garden soil, provided it is not too dry. They need a sunny position, as lack of sunlight results in poor flowering. Plant deutzias while they are dormant, in autumn and early spring. Container-grown plants can be planted throughout the growing season. Cut back flowered wood as low to the ground as possible to encourage strong new flowering shoots. Deutzias can be damaged by frost during severe winters, but quickly make new growth after they have been pruned.

The quick-growing species are propagated from hardwood cuttings. Other species and cultivars are propagated from softwood cuttings inserted in a shaded bed in a greenhouse at the end of May or in June.

Deutzia × rosea was produced by crossing *D. gracilis* with *D. purpurascens*. It is a compact shrub up to 1.5 m (5 ft) high. It makes a handsome specimen in a lawn or in a bed of mat-forming perennials.

D. gracilis is an upright shrub from Japan. Its low height (about 1 m [3¹/₄ ft]) makes it suitable for low, unclipped hedges. Its pure white flowers in upright panicles appear in May and June. Plants grown in large containers can be forced to produce flowering sprigs for cutting.

3

Deutzia × rosea (1, 2) has lanceolate leaves up to 8 cm (3¹/₄ in) long and hairless on the underside. Its wide-open, bell-shaped flowers appear in June. They are about 20 mm (³/₄ in) wide, white, tinted pink on the outer margins of the petals and arranged in sparse panicles. The fruit is a dehiscent capsule formed of 3—5 valves which split apart after it ripens (3).

The most widely grown of the many cultivars are: 'Campanulata' with pure white, cup-shaped flowers in dense panicles; 'Carminea' whose flowers have white centres and deep pink margins; 'Grandiflora' with white flowers up to 30 mm (1¹/₄ in) across, tinted pink on the margins and 'Venusta' with white flowers.

Deutzia
Deutzia scabra
(syn. *D. crenata*)

Saxifragaceae

This Deutzia is a popular plant of gardens and parks. It looks well planted singly or in groups of various sizes and is also suitable for informal hedges.

D. × hybrida is a cross between *D. discolor* and *D. longifolia*, making a shrub about 1.5 m (5 ft) high with leaves larger than those of the species. In June it produces wide-open mallow-pink flowers. The various garden forms include: 'Contraste' with slightly pendent branches and large flowers with wavy petals; 'Magicien' with darker undersides and white-rimmed petals and 'Mont Rose' with large, single, wavy, mallow-pink flowers with yellow anthers.

D. × magnifica was produced by crossing *D. scabra* with *D. vilmoriniae*. It is a shrub of upright habit, growing up to 2 m (6½ ft) high. Its lanceolate leaves are up to 12 cm (4¾ in) long. The rose-shaped pure white flowers are arranged in dense panicles and produced from May to June. Most commonly grown of the many cultivars are: 'Longipetala' with long-petalled white flowers and 'Macrothyrsa' with large clusters of white flowers.

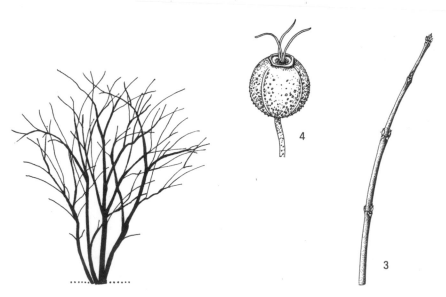

4

3

2

1

Deutzia scabra grows wild in China and Japan. It is an upright shrub about 2.5 m (8¹/₂ ft) high. Its grey shoots (3) turn red-brown when mature. The bark peels off in flakes. The leaves are lanceolate-ovate, up to 15 cm (6 in) long, rough and hairy on both sides. The flowers are borne from June to July and measure about 20 cm (³/₄ in) across. They are arranged in upright panicles (1) up to 13 cm (5 in) long. The fruits (capsules) (4) ripen in October. Good cultivars are 'Candidissima' with pure white, fully double flowers; 'Plena' (2) with double flowers consisting of white petals with a pink tinge on the outside and 'Watereri' with particularly large, single white flowers.

Oleaster, Wild Olive
Elaeagnus commutata

Elaeagnaceae

Oleasters are shrubs or trees with spiny or spineless branchlets. The alternate leaves are covered with silvery scales. Oleasters can be planted as single specimens or in groups. The deciduous species have no special requirements except for sun. They will tolerate quite dry and salty soils and atmospheric pollution and their shoots do not attract wild animals. The roots carry nitrogen-fixing bacteria so the plant can assimilate nitrogen directly from the air. Oleasters need no regular pruning. Cut out only dead shoots, those damaged by frost or which are causing overcrowding. The species are raised from seeds, which can be sown in autumn or stratified and sown the following spring. Propagation by layers or suckers is also possible.

E. angustifolia grows in the Mediterranean region, Turkey and southern parts of the USSR. It is a shrub of irregular shape, reaching a height of about 7 m (23 ft). It does not produce underground suckers. Its narrow, lanceolate, grey-green leaves with silvery undersides are up to 10 cm (4 in) long and persist on the branches into late autumn. The flowers, opening in May and June, are very fragrant, bell-shaped, silvery-white with yellow centres.

E. pungens is an evergreen shrub up to 2 m (6¹/₂ ft) high, which originated in northern China and Japan. Its elliptic leaves are about 10 cm (4 in) long. The inconspicuous flowers appear in October. Its cultivar 'Maculata' has bold yellow splashes on its rich green leaves and has become a popular foliage shrub, cheerful to look at all year round.

2

Elaeagnus commutata (1) is native to
North America. It is an upright,
deciduous shrub up to 3 m (10 ft) high,
which produces many underground
suckers. Its spineless branches with
brown scales carry ovate-lanceolate

1

leaves up to 10 cm (4 in) long. The very
fragrant, yellow flowers suffused with
silver outside open in June. They
develop into silvery fruits (2) with mealy
pulp, measuring about 1 cm ($^3/_8$ in)
long.

European Spindle Tree
Euonymus europaeus

Celastraceae

The European Spindle Tree is used to best effect in large landscaping schemes, often being planted under taller trees. It also makes a good informal garden hedge. It is a hardy woody plant, happy in any fertile soil, provided it is not too dry. It grows best in semi-shade and tolerates a polluted atmosphere.

Spindle Trees are planted in autumn and spring and need no regular pruning. The species are propagated from stratified seeds in spring, the cultivars by summer cuttings under mist propagation.

E. alatus is an east-Asian shrub growing up to 3 m (10 ft) high with four-winged corky bark and leaves that turn a magnificent bright red in the autumn. The carmine-red flowers are followed by small fruits. In our climatic conditions this species only flowers and fruits occassionally.

E. phellomanus is a shrub up to 4 m (13 ft) high, occurring widely in North-western China. The branches have thick corky wings. The elongated, lanceolate leaves turn yellow-red before they fall. The blackish seeds are enclosed in coral-red arils.

The European Spindle Tree (1) is native to Europe and Western Asia, where it grows in fertile soils in thin woodland and on river banks. It is an upright shrub or tree about 4 m (13 ft) high. The edges of older branches are often extended into four black-violet wings. The lanceolate-ovate leaves are up to

2

3

96

1

2

8 cm (3¹/₄ in) long, turning yellow-red in the autumn. The umbels of greenish white flowers open in May. The fruit is a fleshy, pinkish red capsule (2), rather like a bishop's cap. It is formed of four valves, each containing 1—2 oval seeds (3) covered with an orange coat.

The cultivars offered by specialist nurseries differ in the shape and colouring of the leaves as well as in the size and colour of the fruits. They include, for example, 'Aldenhamensis', with pinkish red fruits carried on long stalks; 'Atrorubens' with carmine-red arils and 'Red Cascade' with a profusion of opal-pink fruits.

97

Pearl Bush
Exochorda racemosa
(syn. *E. grandiflora*)

Rosaceae

Pearl Bushes look best when given ample space. This is why they are most frequently planted as solitary subjects or in small groups. They do best in a humus-rich, well-drained soil, but generally do well even in rather dry positions. They thrive in full sun, but tolerate partial shade, though they flower less profusely there.

Prune after flowering by thinning out the oldest branches to encourage new growth and to maintain a compact shape. Pearl Bushes are generally planted while dormant, in autumn and early spring. The species is raised from stratified seeds in spring, the garden forms from layers or summer cuttings.

E. giraldii is a shrub up to 3 m (10 ft) high, which came from North-eastern China. The new shoots are red-brown with fine lenticels. The dark grey mature branches carry obovate leaves up to 6 cm (2¹/₄ in) long. The white flowers with narrow petals appear in May. The variety *wilsonii* has larger leaves and flowers profusely as early as the end of April.

E. korolkowii (syn. *E. albertii*) comes from the mountain slopes of Central Asia. It is a slender shrub up to 5 m (17 ft) high. The leaves with rounded apices measure about 9 cm (3¹/₂ in) long. In May it produces white flowers arranged in clusters up to 8 cm (3¹/₄ in) long.

E. × macrantha is a hybrid between *B. korolkowii* and *E. racemosa*, growing to a height of 3—4 m (10—13 ft). It flowers more profusely than its parents, with larger flowers arranged in dense racemes.

The Pearl Bush comes from Eastern China, where it grows up to 3 m (10 ft) high. It is a wide-spreading deciduous shrub with arching branches. The red-brown shoots are covered with prominent lenticels (4). The leaves are alternate, lanceolate-ovate, slightly wavy and light green with darker undersides. They are about 8 cm (3¹/₄ in) long. The pure white flowers do not have a particularly pleasant scent. Six to nine of them are arranged in each narrow raceme (1) on the previous year's shoots. Each flower has five petals and measures about 4 cm (1¹/₂ in) across. Five-sided capsules are produced after flowering (2). When mature they turn brown, remain on the shrub and split into five parts as late as the following spring (3).

The cultivar 'Irish Pearl' was produced by hybridising *E. racemosa* with *E. giraldii* var. *wilsonii*. Eight to ten of its pure white star-shaped flowers about 5 cm (2 in) across are arranged in each raceme.

1

4

2

3

Golden Bell Tree
Forsythia × intermedia   Oleaceae

The *Forsythia* genus comprises seven species, of which only one is native to Europe, the others to eastern Asia. They are medium-sized shrubs with hollow stems. They flower before the leaves appear on previous year's shoots. They are happy in any garden soil provided it is not too dry, but flower less profusely in shade. They can stand atmospheric pollution. Thin out old wood after flowering to stimulate the growth of vigorous shoots that will bear masses of flowers the following year. Feed the plant with compound fertilizer solution at the same time. In nurseries forsythias are propagated by hardwood cuttings taken from ripe shoots in the autumn or by softwood cuttings under mist in early summer.

Forsythia × intermedia is a hybrid of *F. suspensa* and *F. viridissima*. It was discovered in Göttingen Botanical Garden, Germany, in 1878. It makes a lovely specimen shrub for a small garden. Forsythias are often planted in groups in parks and on modern housing estates. They are sometimes used for clipped hedges and grown in shallow bowls by bonsai growers. From December onwards the twigs can be cut and put in vases, where they will soon flower provided they weren't cut before the first frost.

Forsythia × intermedia (1) is an erect shrub with spreading branches, growing about 2—3 m (6¹/₂—10 ft) high. Its yellow-brown shoots (2) carry narrow elliptic leaves up to 12 cm (4³/₄ in) long (3). The bright yellow flowers with long stigmas are produced in late March and April. They are borne in twos or threes in axillary clusters. The fruits are dehiscent, two-valved capsules,

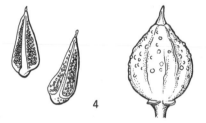

4

3

containing many winged seeds (4).

The most widely grown cultivars are: 'Beatrix Farrand' (5) with chrome-yellow flowers up to 6 cm (2¹/₄ in) long; 'Lynwood' with golden-yellow flowers with wide petals borne along the branchlets; 'Primulina' with primrose-yellow flowers with narrow, curly edges; 'Spectabilis' with golden-yellow flowers appearing in March and 'Vitellina', with a profusion of rather small, butter-yellow flowers.

Forsythia suspensa is often planted on steep slopes, as its arching branches are quick to root when they touch the ground.

F. ovata is a Korean species up to 2 m (6¹/₂ ft) high. The new shoots are grey-yellow, the oval leaves measure up to 7 cm (2³/₄ in) long. This species does not flower as profusely as the other forsythias and its primrose-yellow flowers are rather small. On the other hand, it flowers about two weeks earlier than the other species and varieties, during March. Nurseries also offer the cultivar 'Robusta' with butter-yellow flowers.

F. viridissima is native to the mountain slopes of Central and Eastern China. It is an erect shrub about 3 m (10 ft) high. Its quadrangular, olive-green shoots are covered with wartlike lenticels. The leaves are narrow and elliptic, turning brown-violet in autumn. The yellow-green flowers with long curled-back petals are produced rather late, in April. Winter protection is essential in cold areas. The cultivar 'Bronxensis' is only 30 cm (1 ft) high. It makes a good pot-grown or rock garden shrub, but its flowers are rather sparse.

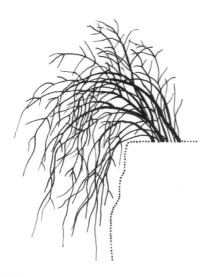

Forsythia suspensa grows wild on the mountain slopes of Northern and Central China and in Japan. It makes a shrub up to 3 m (9¹/₂ ft) high. The light brown shoots (2) are hollow, only the nodes being solid. The leaves are elongate ovate, generally trifoliate, up to 10 cm (2 in) long (1). The sulphur-yellow flowers (3) with short stigmas are usually carried in twos in axillary clusters and open in March. The fruits mature in September.

The variety *fortunei* came from Eastern China. Young plants are erect, the long shoots of mature specimens are pendulous. The long, green-brown young stems carry mostly trifoliate leaves. The dark yellow flowers are borne from late March to April. The

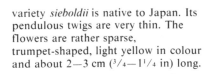

2

1

3

variety *sieboldii* is native to Japan. Its
pendulous twigs are very thin. The
flowers are rather sparse,
trumpet-shaped, light yellow in colour
and about 2—3 cm (³/₄—1¹/₄ in) long.

103

Dyer's Greenweed, Broom
Genista tinctoria   Leguminosae

Genistas look well planted in groups in front of taller shrubs. The low-growing species are also attractive in a bed of perennials, rock or heath garden as well as in landscaped areas. The different species vary in their environmental requirements depending on their origin, but most tolerate quite dry, poor soils. Direct sun is essential. As they form a single taproot, genistas cannot bear replanting. Young plants are best planted with a root ball in spring. Cut back any shoots damaged by frost and the shrub will make new growth from the base. Genistas are raised from stratified seeds sown in trays in March or outdoors in May. This is also the time to take cuttings. Insert these under mist propagation, but they are slow to root even when treated with hormone rooting powder.

Spanish Gorse (*G. hispanica*), is native to northern Spain and southern France. It is a thickly-branched spiny shrub about 40 cm (16 in) high. The golden-yellow flowers in small terminal racemes open from May to July. This shrub may need winter protection.

G. pilosa originates in Western, Northern and Southern Europe, where it grows on rather dry heath soils. It is a prostrate shrub with upright branches, reaching only about 30 cm (1 ft) high. Its small golden-yellow flowers are produced in May and June. This shrub sometimes has a second flowering in September.

G. radiata grows on the southern slopes of the Alps. It is a wide-spreading, radially-branched shrub with hairy, spineless, green branchlets. It grows about 60 cm (2 ft) high. The yellow flowers in racemes of 20 are produced in June. This species requires a warm position.

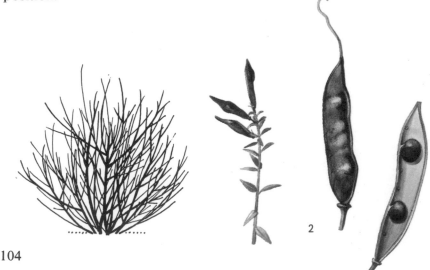

2

Genista tinctoria grows on dry, sandy and limy soils throughout Europe, Turkey and the Caucasus. It is a broom-like shrub about 60 cm (2 ft) high. Its green, grooved, spineless branchlets bear lanceolate, finely hairy leaves up to 3 cm (1¹/₄ in) long. The racemes of yellow flowers (1) are up to 6 cm (2¹/₄ in) long and open in succession from June to August. The fruits are brown pods about 3 cm (1¹/₄ in) long, containing 6—10 seeds (2). The cultivar 'Plena' is only 30 cm (1 ft) high, with golden-yellow flowers flushed with orange. 'Royal Gold' grows up to 80 cm (31¹/₂ in) high, producing a profusion of golden-yellow flowers as late as July.

1

Carolina Silver Bell, Snowdrop Tree
Halesia carolina
(syn. *H. tetraptera*) — Styracaceae

Halesias are North American woody plants, hardy in our conditions, though they need ample sun. They will succeed in any deep, fresh, slightly acid soil. They rarely suffer from pests and diseases and no control is required. Plant container-grown seedlings and keep the rootball intact. No regular pruning is necessary, as this shrub flowers on two-year-old shoots. It is raised in nurseries from stratified seeds. You can also try propagation by cuttings or two-year-old layers.

The Carolina Silver Bell is a graceful shrub, not as widely grown as it deserves. No special care is required, provided it is grown in a warm, south-facing position.

H. diptera grows on river banks and in humid forests in south-eastern parts of the U.S.A., where it makes a tree up to 15 m (50 ft) high. In our conditions it only grows into a shrub. The young shoots covered with grey hairs become smooth and grey-brown as they mature. The coarsely dentate, obovate leaves are finely felted when young, later becoming smooth. The white flowers, each with eight stamens almost as long as the corolla, are produced in May or June. The fruit is a dry, elongated drupe with two wings.

H. monticola is native to the mountain slopes of the north-eastern United States. Its flowers are much larger than those of *H. carolina*, with petals up to 25 mm (1 in) long. The fruits are about 5 cm (2 in) long.

Halesia carolina, a North American species, makes a tree up to 20 m (66 ft) high in its homeland. In Britain it is a spreading shrub about 5 m (17 ft) high, with peeling bark on old twigs (4). The ovate, finely serrate leaves (3) are about 10 cm (4 in) long, covered with hairs when young, but turning smooth when mature. Its autumn foliage is yellow. It flowers before the leaves appear, in late April and early May. The white flowers (1) are bell-shaped, drooping, about 15 mm (⅝ in) long and arranged in clusters of two to five. Each flower has 12—16 stamens, shorter than the corolla (2). The fruit is a dry, elongated drupe which ripens in September, with wide, somewhat wavy wings (5). This species is less hardy than *C. diptera*.

107

Japanese Witch Hazel
Hamamelis japonica

Hamamelidaceae

The genus *Hamamelis* comprises only six species, growing wild in North America and Eastern Asia. Witch hazels are very handsome woody plants and flower when most plants are still dormant, from late winter until early spring, or even in late autumn. This is why they are best planted as solitary subjects or in small groups alongside paths or near arbours so that one could closely watch their graceful flowers. They also look fine in beds of low-growing perennials. The only reason why Witch hazels are not often seen in gardens is that their dry leaves remain on the branches until late winter, partly concealing the flowers. This effect can be reduced by feeding the shrub with 40% potash at 50 g per 1 m² (1¹/₂ oz per sq yd). This will make the shrub shed its leaves earlier.

Witch hazels are happy in any humus-rich fertile soil that is not too dry. They will not tolerate limy soils. They grow best in sheltered positions, but tolerate semi-shade and polluted air. Even if planted with an intact rootball, they are very slow to grow. Older plants do not tolerate replanting. All species are hardy in Britain, though their flowers could be damaged by frost. Witch hazels should not be pruned, though twigs can be cut from large plants for home decoration. Plants are raised from stratified seeds sown in heat. Asian species can be propagated from one-year-old layers. Garden forms are grafted onto *H. virginiana* rootstocks.

The Japanese Witch Hazel grows in the mountain forests of Japan and China. In its homeland it makes a tree with a broad spreading crown and reaches a height of up to 7 m (23 ft). In our conditions it is only about 2.5 m (8¹/₂ ft) high. The leaves are broadly ovate, up to 10 cm (4 in) long, with light undersides. They turn bright red in autumn before they fall. Some leaves are shed as late as spring, just before the new ones appear. This shrub flowers from late winter to early spring, in the most favourable conditions as early as February. The golden-yellow flowers have a red-brown

patterned calyx, and hook-shaped,
slightly wavy petals up to 20 mm ($^3/_4$ in)
long. The fruit is a woody capsule (2)
containing two black seeds. This species
requires a rather sheltered position. The
variety *arborea* has larger dark yellow
flowers with a purple spot inside. The
variety *flavopurpurascens* (1) has reddish
flowers with a purple calyx. The cultivar
'Zucchariniana' has lemon-yellow
flowers with a greenish calyx. It flowers
as late as the end of March.

1

2

Chinese Witch Hazel
Hamamelis mollis

Hamamelidaceae

This species of *Hamamelis* is planted to best effect as specimen shrub in gardens and landscaped areas. It flowers in early spring, when other flowers are rare. Its attractive flowers are not damaged by frost and open while snow is still on the ground.

H. × *intermedia* is a hybrid between *H. japonica* and *H. mollis*, marketed since 1950's. It is a fast-growing shrub about 3—4 m (10—13 ft) high, its shoots covered with grey-brown hairs. Its obovate leaves, whose undersides are covered with fine hairs, are up to 10 cm (4 in) long. The dark yellow flowers are formed of narrow, strap-like petals curled at the tip. This hybrid does not produce seeds, so is propagated by grafting or layering. The following cultivars are most widely offered for sale by specialized nurseries: 'Allgold' with elliptic leaves coloured yellow in autumn, and dark yellow flowers with a red calyx; 'Carmine Red' with carmine-red flowers and yellow autumn foliage; 'Diane' with rather large, carmine-red flowers in dense clusters; 'Hiltingbury' of erect habit with coppery-red flowers and orange-red autumn foliage; 'Jelena' ('Copper Beauty') with curled yellow flowers and wine-red calyx, the leaves turning scarlet in autumn, the flowers produced very early in spring; 'Magic Fire' ('Feuerzauber') with long, curled, coppery-orange petals suffused with red; 'Moonlight' with sulphur-yellow flowers with a red spot at the base and yellow autumn foliage.

Hamamelis mollis (1) is native to the Chinese provinces of Hupei and Kiangsi, where it makes a big bush even at 2,000 m (6,400 ft) above sea level. In our conditions it makes a wide-spreading shrub only about 3 m (10 ft) high. The young shoots (3), buds and leaves are finely grey-felted, the older branches grey-brown and smooth.

The leaves are up to 15 cm (6 in) long, cordate at the base and thickly felted on the underside, with a metallic sheen. They turn golden-yellow in autumn (2).

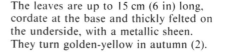

Flowers open mainly in February and March. They are golden-yellow and formed of rather wide, straight petals up to 30 mm (1¼ in) long. The slightly fragrant calyx is brown-felted outside and purple inside. The cultivar 'Brevipetala' flowers very early with small orange-yellow blossoms arranged in dense clusters. 'Pallida' has fragrant, light yellow flowers with wavy petals and wine-red calyx.

111

Hamamelis virginiana flowers as early as October and November in our climate. Unfortunately, its leaves hang on and rather diminish its ornamental value, though it still makes a delightful specimen shrub.

H. vernalis, the Ozark Witch Hazel, has not been widely grown yet. It is a native of North America, where it grows on inundated river banks. It reaches a maximum height of 2 m (6^1/$_2$ ft) and produces plenty of underground suckers. The young shoots are covered with thick hairs, older branches are grey-brown, horizontally and vertically wrinkled. The obovate leaves are grey-green on the underside and up to 12 cm (4^3/$_4$ in) long. Its autumn foliage is a magnificent orange-red. In favourable weather conditions it produces a profusion of fragrant flowers from January to March. They are rather small, with a reddish calyx and light yellow petals about 6 mm (^{1}/$_4$ in) long. This species requires a warm sheltered position. The cultivar 'Red Imp' produces bright red flowers with a darker spot on the calyx. 'Sandra' has cadmium-yellow petals and orange or red-coloured autumn foliage. 'Squib' has yellow petals and a green calyx.

H. macrophylla originates from the South-eastern United States. It is a shrub of broadly spreading habit or a small tree. Its ovate leaves are wrinkled and finely hairy, turning butter-yellow in autumn. The tiny yellow flowers are produced from December to February in favourable climatic conditions.

Hamamelis virginiana grows wild in alluvial soils in the eastern parts of the United States. It is a shrub up to 5 m (17 ft) high. Its broom-shaped red-brown shoots are finely felted. Older branches are grey and hairless with numerous lenticels. The obovate leaves (2) are asymmetrical, coarsely wrinkled, with six pairs of veins. They are up to 12 cm (4^3/$_4$ in) long and soon become hairless on both sides. They turn yellow in autumn before they fall (3). The light yellow flowers (1) are rather small; the yellow-brown centre of the calyx becomes greenish after flowering. The flowers are very fragrant. In spring they develop into tetrahedral, two-valved, grey-felted capsules (4) about 1 cm

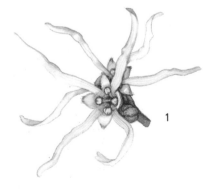

1

2

3

4

(³/₈ in) long. Though the two valves split
open, they persist on the branches till
autumn. Each capsule contains two
elongated seeds that are dispersed
nearby when ripe.

Rose Mallow
Hibiscus syriacus

Malvaceae

In gardens Rose Mallows are usually planted as single specimens, but in parks are best planted in small groups. In warm sunny districts they are used to make hedges. They thrive in a sunny, warm and sheltered position with deep, well-drained and humus-rich soil. They are best planted in spring so they have time to spread their roots before winter. They need winter protection in harsher areas. Tying up the top growth and covering them with green brushwood is usually sufficient. If the plants are damaged by air frosts, cut them hard back in early spring. They will soon make new growth from the roots. Before the frosts arrive cover the soil above the roots with a layer of dry foliage and green brushwood. In cold districts the shrub is best potted in a large container and kept in a cool room for the winter. Prune back old plants to two to five buds in late winter to encourage the growth of strong, new flowering shoots. The cultivars are grafted onto *H. syriacus* seedlings in late winter in a greenhouse. The species is raised from seeds sown in a warmed frame in spring. Softwood cuttings are slow to root.

The original Rose Mallow species is no longer grown now that many garden forms have been bred in Britain and France. They give white, pink, red, violet and blue flowers. Cultivars with single flowers are preferable, as semi-double and double flowers are liable to rot during rainy periods in summer.

Hibiscus syriacus is not native to Syria, as its name suggests, but to India and China, where it has been grown as an ornamental plant for centuries. It is a shrub of strictly erect habit. In Britain it reaches a height of about 2 m (6½ ft), but in more favourable climates grows twice as high. The young shoots are

3

grey-green and finely felted, older branches ash-grey with lighter lenticels. It flowers on current season's shoots. The bell-shaped flowers about 6 cm (2¹/₄ in) across are borne in axillary

spurs. The species has light violet flowers with a darker spot at the base of the petals. The fruit is a capsule formed of five valves containing many black seeds (4). The most popular cultivars are 'Blue Bird' (2), lilac blue, single; 'Hamabo', lilac pink, single; 'Lady Stanley' (1), pinkish with a red spot; 'Woodbridge' (3), ruby-red, single, and 'William R. Smith', pure white, single.

115

Sea Buckthorn
Hippophaë rhamnoides   Elaeagnaceae

Sea Buckthorns make attractive specimen shrubs in small gardens, but they are unisexual and need both male and female plants to form fruits. This is why in large gardens and parks they are mostly planted in groups of five females to one male plant. A male plant can be distinguished by its larger and more numerous buds compared with the female. Its wide-spreading root system makes the Sea Buckthorn valuable for anchoring crumbly soil on hillsides, as it produces many suckers. It is also a popular pot-grown shrub.

H. rhamnoides thrives in a well-drained, fairly dry and limy soil in full sun. It tolerates salty soils and a polluted atmosphere. The nitrogen-fixing bacteria on its roots enable it to assimilate nitrogen straight from the air. It is fully hardy in Britain.

It is best planted in spring so the plant can spread its roots before the winter. Keep the root ball intact. Plants more then three years old are slow to take. In nurseries Sea Buckthorns are grown from stratified seeds sown in the open ground in spring. A smaller number of young plants is obtained from suckers or hardwood cuttings taken from one-year-old shoots.

H. salicifolia comes from the slopes of the Himalayas. It is a shrub or tree up to 6 m (20 ft) high with pendulous branches, which are less spiny than those of the Sea Buckthorn. The small, inconspicuous flowers open in March and April. The fruits are yellow berries about the size of a pea. This species is rarely seen in cultivation.

Sea Buckthorn is distributed throughout Europe and across to Northern China. It is a common plant of sea coast and river banks. It is a sparsely-branched, spiny shrub or tree (3), growing up to 5 m (17 ft) high. The young shoots are yellow-brown and glossy, turning dark brown as the plant matures. The golden brown buds are also ornamental. They open to reveal narrow, lanceolate leaves (4) up to 7 cm (2³/₄ in) long, with white-felted undersides and rusty-red midribs. The small, dull yellow flowers (5) are dioecious (unisexual) and appear before the leaves in early April. Female flowers are separate, trumpet-shaped, with protruding styles. Male flowers are arranged in short racemes on the undersides of the shoots. They are

ovate-spherical, sessile or short-stalked,
two-part and deeply cleft. The
orange-red fruits with hard oval seeds
(1, 2) are about 7 mm (2³/₄ in) long, are
rich in vitamin C and can be used to
make juices and preserves.

Hydrangea arborescens Saxifragaceae

The genus *Hydrangea* comprises 23 species, growing in temperate and sub-tropical parts of South-eastern Asia and North America. The species are very variable, some species and garden forms making delightful specimen shrubs, that look well planted in grass or among perennials. Other species are most attractive planted in compact or open groupings. In favourable climatic conditions hydrangeas make lovely informal flowering hedges. They are also very decorative in tubs and other containers.

All Hydrangea species thrive in semi-shade, but if supplied with enough moisture can bear full sunlight as well. They grow best in a humus-rich nourishing, fairly acid soil. The large leaves transpire large amounts of water, so regular watering is essential in a hot summer. They tolerate somewhat polluted air. Plant them in late spring to avoid frost damage, but early enough for them to become established before winter arrives. Most species are better not pruned at all, for they flower on the previous year's shoots. Only prune back the aerial parts damaged by frost to encourage new growth from the roots. Protect the shrub with straw held in place with plastic netting the first winter after planting out.

Hydrangeas are generally propagated by softwood cuttings taken from June to August. Treat them with hormone rooting powder and insert in a propagator or warmed frame. Plant in the open the following spring. They can also be propagated from suckers and root cuttings.

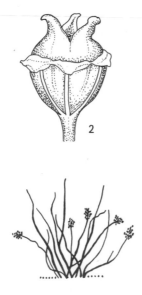

Hydrangea arborescens grows wild in the damp forests and on river banks in the eastern United States. It is a spreading shrub up to 2 m (6¹/₂ ft) high. The shoots are grey-brown, older branches brown with the bark flaking off. The broadly ovate leaves are up to 18 cm (7 in) long. The green-white flowers arranged in flat corymbs about 10 cm (4 in) across open from July to August. The fruit is a capsule with five valves (2), each containing many small, yellow-brown seeds, which ripen in September and October.

The species is no longer cultivated, as more attractive cultivars have been bred. 'Grandiflora' produces sterile, green-white flowers (1) arranged in hemispherical inflorescences up to 20 cm (8 in) wide. It flowers from July to September.

1

♀

♂

Hydrangea paniculata is a popular shrub, as it is one of the few which flower in mid and late summer. The tree-like forms make pot-grown plants.

Sargent's Hydrangea (*H. sargentiana*), is native to Central China. It is a shrub 2 m (6¹/₂ ft) high, with branchlets densely covered with hairs and heart-shaped leaves up to 25 cm (10 in) long, grey-white felted beneath. The flowers in inflorescences about 20 cm (8 in) across are produced in July and August. They are steel-blue, the florets round the edge being sterile and white.

H. macrophylla grows wild in the Himalayas, Southern China and Japan, where it reaches a height of about 3 m (10 ft). In our conditions it barely reaches 1.5 m (5 ft) high. The shoots are green, spotted with brown. The leaves are hairless, broadly ovate, pointed and up to 20 cm (8 in) long. They turn red-brown in autumn. Flowering time is from June to August. The flowers appear in flat umbels up to 20 cm (8 in) across with white, hermaphrodite, fertile flowers in the centre and white, pink or pale blue sterile florets around the margin. The colouring varies according to the soil reaction. Pink cultivars produce blue flowers in acid soils and red in alkaline soils. Only white cultivars do not change the colour of their flowers. Blue-coloured flowers can be produced on pink cultivars by adding 3 g of alum to 1 litre of water used for watering. Flowered pot-grown hydrangeas used to be planted out in the open, but modern large-flowered cultivars are no longer suitable for this purpose. But they can be grown in large containers and stood on a terrace or patio for the summer.

Hydrangea paniculata grows wild in Japan, South-eastern China and on the Sakhalin and Kurile Islands. It grows up to 3 m (10 ft) high in our conditions.

The shoots (2) are green, covered with hairs. Older branches are hairless with peeling, grey-brown bark. The elliptic leaves are up to 15 cm (6 in) long, light green beneath, with fluffy hairs on the veins. The flowers are arranged in conical, terminal panicles about 25 cm (10 in) long, most of them sterile. They

4

appear in August and are white, aging to dark pink. Most commonly grown is the cultivar 'Grandiflora' (1) with panicles up to 30 cm (1 ft) long, composed exclusively of sterile white florets later turning pinkish red (3). The fruit is a many-seeded capsule (4). 'Praecox' produces shorter panicles of flowers, but blooms as early as the beginning of July.

1

2

3

Rose of Sharon, St John's Wort
Hypericum patulum

Guttiferae

Hypericum is a popular woody plant used in place of grass to carpet large areas or planted in a rockery or heather garden. It needs a deep, humus-rich, moist soil, but does equally well in full sun or semi-shade. A thin winter covering of green brushwood will protect the plant from the untimely onset of growth in a mild winter or from frost damage. After a severe winter cut back the damaged shoots. It will rapidly make new growth from the roots.

The Rose of Sharon, *H. calycinum*, is best planted with a ball of roots in spring. Scythe the shoots of the sub-shrubby species in the autumn and leave them on the ground as a winter covering. The shrubby species require no pruning. They are propagated from softwood cuttings taken preferably in July. Sub-shrubby kinds are increased by dividing the clumps in spring or autumn.

H. hookeranum is native to Southern India and Western China. It is a semi-evergreen species up to 1 m (3¼ ft) high. Its yellow, plate-like flowers arranged in terminal inflorescences appear in September.

H. × moseranum was produced by crossing *H. calycinum* with *H. patulum*. It is a semi-evergreen shrub only 50 cm (20 in) high, which produces no underground shoots. The ovate leaves are about 5 cm (2 in) long. The golden-yellow flowers up to 6 cm (2¼ in) across open in succession from July to October.

H. androsaeum (Tutsan) grows in western and southern Europe, North Africa, Turkey and the Caucasus, making a semi-evergreen shrub up to 1 m (3¼ ft) high. Its small, golden-yellow flowers are borne from July to September. They are followed by globular, red-brown fruits, which age to black.

2

122

H. patulum is native to Japan and China. It is a shrub up to 1 m (3¹/₄ ft) high with ovate-lanceolate leaves about 5 cm (2 in) long. In bleak areas it requires a sheltered spot. The most commonly grown cultivar 'Hidcote' is up to 1.5 m (5 ft) high. Its golden-yellow flowers (1) about 6 cm (2¹/₄ in) across open in succession from July to October and are followed by many-seeded capsules (2) that ripen in October and November.

1

Common Holly
Ilex aquifolium

Hollies are planted as single specimens in small gardens. In large gardens and parks they look attractive planted in groups in front of sparse trees or shrubs. They also make good informal or trimmed hedges. Cut twigs last a long time in a vase and are highly decorative.

Holly grows best near the sea where the air is humid. There it tolerates direct sunlight, but in a continental climate it should be planted in partial shade sheltered from winter sun. It does best in humus-rich, heavy moist soils but easily adapts to the most varied soil and climatic conditions. It is best planted with the root ball, preferably just after its new leaves have sprouted. Cut back any shoots which have been damaged by frost to encourage new growth. Young plants are better covered with a peat layer, dead leaves or green brushwood before frosts arrive. The species are raised from stratified seeds sown outdoors in spring. The cultivars are propagated from cuttings taken preferably in July and August. They can also be propagated by layering low-growing shoots.

I. verticillata is native to humid North American lowlands and borders of deciduous forests. It is a shrub about 2 m (6½ ft) high with deciduous, broadly ovate leaves pointed at each end. The yellowish flowers open in June and develop into the globular, orange-red fruits which remain on the branches throughout the winter. This species is only suitable for mild areas.

Common Holly (1) grows wild in southern and western Europe and across into Iran. In a favourable climate it forms a tree up to 10 m (33 ft) high, but in our conditions even a 100-year-old tree is barely half that size. Its evergreen leaves with wavy and prickly margins and lighter undersides are up to 8 cm (3¼ in) long. The creamy white flowers up to 1 cm (⅜ in) across are very

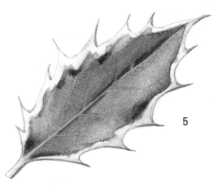

5

fragrant. They are produced from May to June on the previous year's growth. Two to six male flowers (2) are borne in each axillary spur, female ones (2) are separate. The fruits (3) — coral-red drupes containing two to four kernels (4) mature in October.

Cultivars commonly found in cultivation include: 'Golden Queen' bearing leaves with golden-yellow margins; 'Argenteomarginata' (5), broad leaves with white margins; 'J. C. van Tol', ovate leaves up to 7 cm (2³/₄ in) long and a profusion of fruits, and 'Pyramidalis', free fruiting with green foliage.

Jew's Mallow
Kerria japonica
Rosaceae

Kerrias are planted singly or in groups, perhaps mixed with other shrubs, in both large and small gardens. They look striking in front of taller trees and can also be used to form unclipped hedges.

Kerrias thrive in any normal garden soil, provided it is not extremely dry. They can bear direct sunlight or semi-shade, but become stunted in deep shade and do not flower. They tolerate polluted town air and stand up well to our winters. The soft shoot tips may be damaged by frost, but quickly make new growth when cut back in spring.

In sandy soil kerrias produce many underground suckers and tend to spread too far. To keep them the right size and shape, cut back the oldest flowered branches to ground level.

Amateurs propagate kerrias by careful division of underground suckers, but propagation by softwood cuttings, inserted in frames in June and July is more productive.

Kerria japonica (1) is native to China, but is nowadays widely distributed throughout eastern Asia and occasionally even in Europe, where it was introduced in 1700. It is a deciduous shrub about 1.5 m (5 ft) high, producing many sparsely-branched, glossy green shoots (3). Older branches are grey-green. They bear alternate, ovate leaves with an elongated tip. They measure about 2—5 cm (3/4—2 in) long and turn golden-yellow in autumn before they fall. The flowering period is from May to June, but the shrub may flower for a second time in the autumn. The single, golden-yellow flowers (4) are about 4 cm (1 1/2 in) wide. The black-brown samaras about 10 cm (4 in) long ripen in September. Each fruit contains four to six brownish-yellow, reniform seeds.

The cultivar 'Pleniflora' — Bachelor's Buttons (2) — makes more compact growth. It does not spread so wide, but it is rather tall — up to 2.5 m (8 1/2 ft). Its double, golden-yellow flowers are up to 5 cm (2 in) across. This cultivar is more tender than the species itself. Also grown is 'Picta' with white-edged grey-green leaves. It is a slow-grower and flowers less profusely than the species.

4

2

1

3

127

Beauty Bush
Kolkwitzia amabilis

Caprifoliaceae

The Beauty Bush is spectacular in flower, but unfortunately is seldom found in our gardens. Kolkwitzia can be planted as a solitary specimen shrub on a lawn or in a bed of low-growing perennials. In a large garden or park it can be planted in groups alongside a fence or in front of taller woody plants. It is also a good pot-grown shrub.

Kolkwitzia grows well in a fairly warm sunny position or in light shade. It does best in rather light porous soil containing ample plant food. It will even thrive on dryish slopes and stands up quite well to a polluted atmosphere.

Best time for planting is spring, even for container-grown seedlings bought from a nursery. Cover the soil over its roots with a mulch of peat or processed bark during its first year after planting. Any shoots which are damaged by air frost should be cut back to encourage rapid new growth. Otherwise limit pruning to occasional thinning out or removing the oldest branches.

In nurseries kolkwitzias are raised from seeds in spring. The seeds are sown in shallow trays in a greenhouse or heated frame. You can also propagate them from softwood cuttings, which root quite rapidly even in an unheated propagator. Kolkwitzias grow rather slowly in the first couple of years after planting, producing their first heavy crop of flowers several years later.

Kolkwitzia amabilis (1) is native to the Chinese provinces of Hupei and Shensi. It is a thickly-branched, deciduous shrub with arching branches about 2 m (6¹/₂ ft) high. The new shoots (2) are clothed with thick hairs, older branches are hairless, reddish-brown with peeling bark. The broadly-ovate leaves are up to

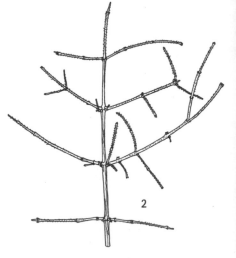

128

7 cm (2³/₄ in) long, turning red-brown in autumn. The bell-shaped flowers in corymbs bloom in May and June on the previous year's shoots. The sweetly-scented flowers are pink-white with a yellow mouth and about 15 mm (⁵/₈ in) long.

In full bloom this shrub is covered with so many flowers that the leaves are obscured. The fruits — one-seeded capsules with conspicuous bristles — carry the remnants of sepals (3). Widely grown are the cultivars 'Pink Cloud' with deep pink flowers and 'Rosea' with rosy-red flowers without the yellow spot in the mouth.

Common Laburnum, Golden Rain
Laburnum anagyroides
(syn. *L. vulgare)*

Leguminosae

Laburnum looks well planted as a specimen tree in parks and gardens, but is also good for mixed groupings. It requires a warm aspect, full sun or only light shade. It thrives in fairly light, well-drained soil and does quite well even in a polluted environment. It is fully hardy in Britain. Do not cut the plant hard back. Raise it from seeds sown in mid-autumn. They will germinate the following spring. The hybrid *L. × watereri* and cultivars are propagated by hardwood cuttings in early October, by summer cuttings in mid-July, by budding in the summer and by grafting on to *L. anagyroides* seedlings in spring.

The Scotch Laburnum (*L. alpinum*), grows wild on Alpine slopes, where it reaches a height of 5 m (17 ft). Its long, smooth, yellow-green shoots carry trifoliate leaves. The leaflets are covered with thin hairs and measure up to 7 cm (2³/₄ in) long. The fragrant, pale yellow flowers without the brown spots typical of the Common Laburnum are arranged in racemes up to 30 cm (1 ft) long. This laburnum flowers in June.

L. × watereri is a hybrid between *L. alpinum* and *L. anagyroides*. Its leaflets are light green, the hairs thinner. The fragrant flowers are a light golden-yellow, finely striped at the base. They are arranged in racemes up to 40 cm (16 in) long. The most commonly grown cultivar, 'Vossii', grows about 3—5 m (10—17 ft) high and bears a profusion of golden-yellow flowers in racemes up to 50 cm (20 in) long.

The Common Laburnum (1) originated in Southern Europe, but spread spontaneously to the warmer parts of Central Europe. It is a wide-spreading shrub or tree up to 6 m (20 ft) high. Its grey-green shoots (2) are silver-felted when young, later turning smooth and brownish. Its trifoliate leaves are formed of leaflets about 8 cm (3¹/₄ in) long. The flowers appear from mid-May to late June in racemes up to 25 cm (10 in) long containing 10—40 rich yellow flowers with a striking brown pattern at the base. The fruits are sickle-shaped, silver-felted pods (3) up to 8 cm (3¹/₄ in) long containing black-brown, kidney-shaped seeds (4), each measuring about 3 mm (¹/₈ in). They mature in late

4

1

2

3

October. The cultivars most frequently
found in cultivation include 'Aureum',
'Autumnale', 'Erecta', 'Pendulum' and
'Quercifolium'.

CAUTION: All parts of this plant are
poisonous. They contain the alkaloids
cytisin and choline, which can be fatal
when eaten in large amounts.

Privet
Ligustrum ovalifolium
Oleaceae

The genus *Ligustrum* contains some 50 species, most distributed through Eastern Asia. Only one species (see following two pages) is native to Europe. Privets are good woody plants for clipped and uncut hedges of various heights, as they stand up well to regular pruning. They are also used for underplanting taller trees in large gardens and parks. They thrive in full sun as well as partial shade and will tolerate even quite deep shade and polluted atmospheres. They do well in any garden soil that is not too waterlogged. The evergreen species are less hardy and require warmer situations.

Formal hedges should be clipped in autumn and during the period of vigorous growth in spring. Try to start pruning immediately after planting to achieve thick branching from the base.

The species are propagated from seeds, which are stratified in May and then sown in November. However, the most common method is by hardwood cuttings taken in autumn. Slow-growing cultivars can be propagated from softwood cuttings inserted in a propagator between June and August. *L. ovalifolium* and its variegated cultivars can also be bought in containers.

Ligustrum ovalifolium (1) is native to Southern and Central Japan, where it grows up to a height of 6 m (20 ft). In Britain it is much smaller, as its young shoots can be damaged by frost.

The broadly elliptic, dark green leaves up to 7 cm ($2^3/_4$ in) long remain on the shrub only in fairly mild sheltered places. The creamy white flowers in terminal panicles up to 10 cm (4 in) long open in July. Most commonly grown are the garden forms 'Aureum' with yellow margins to the leaves (2) and 'Argenteomarginatum' with white-splashed leaves. They are rather low and grow more slowly than the species.

CAUTION: The fruits, globular black berries, are extremely poisonous, so this shrub is not a good choice for gardens where children play.

1

2

133

Common Privet
Ligustrum vulgare   Oleaceae

Common Privet is usually grown to make formal hedges about 1.5 m (5 ft) high. It is fully hardy in Britain.

L. amurense, a native of northern China, is an erect shrub reaching a height of 3 m (10 ft). Its young shoots are covered with fine hairs, the hairless, elliptic leaves up to 8 cm (3¹/₄ in) long are shed in the early winter. The profuse flowers are produced in June and July. The fruits are oval black berries.

L. obtusifolium is native to Japan, Northern China and Korea. It is a deciduous shrub about 2 m (6¹/₂ ft) high with arching shoots clothed with fine hairs. The ovate-lanceolate leaves are covered with sparse hairs and measure up to 8 cm (3¹/₄ in) long. The flowers open in June. The fruits are globular black berries with a grey bloom.

L. sinense is a Chinese species reaching a height of almost 4 m (13 ft) in its homeland. In Britain it is much smaller. The hairless shoots have fine lenticels, the elliptic leaves with pointed tips are up to 7 cm (2³/₄ in) long and in sheltered places remain on the shrub into the winter. The panicles of fragrant flowers are up to 10 cm (4 in) long and open in July and August. The fruits are black-red berries.

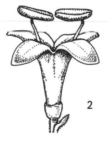

2

Common Privet (1) grows wild in Europe, Asia and North Africa. It is an erect, thickly-branched shrub up to 4 m (13 ft) high. The grey-green shoots with brownish lenticels are rather long; older branches turn grey-brown. The ovate-lanceolate leaves about 6 cm (2¹/₄ in) long may be shed in late autumn in harsh conditions. The upright flower panicles 6—8 cm (2¹/₄—3¹/₄ in)

4

long are formed of small white flowers
(2) opening in June and July. The
globular black berries (3) ripen in
October. Each berry contains two
elongated violet-brown seeds (4)
enclosed in membranous chambers. The
fruits, which are poisonous like those of
L. ovalifolium, remain on the branches
throughout winter, unless eaten by birds.

Tulip Tree
Liriodendron tulipifera
Magnoliaceae

Tulip Trees are more often encountered in parks and avenues than in gardens, though they make delightful specimen trees for large gardens. In favourable situations they are well branched from the very bottom.

Tulip Trees require a deep loamy soil with ample moisture and nutrients. They do not tolerate limy soils, so be sure to choose a position with an acid to neutral soil. They need plenty of light and are happy in warm situations, though older plants stand up well to frost even in our climate. They also tolerate smoky atmosphere in industrial districts.

Plant Tulip Trees in spring, preferably when the young shoots begin to sprout. Be careful not to disturb the root ball when planting a container-grown plant. Protect the fleshy roots from becoming too dry and brittle. Mature trees will not tolerate replanting.

Specialist nurseries propagate Tulip Trees from imported seeds sown under glass in autumn or stratified and sown the following spring. The lower branches can be layered. They are rather slow to root, so should not be severed from the mother plant for at least two or three years after rooting. Garden forms are grafted on to potted seedlings of the same species in a greenhouse in winter.

Liriodendron tulipifera (1), a North American species, reaches a height of 60 m (190 ft) in its homeland, but it can sometimes be seen in gardens as a large shrub. The young stems (2) are grey-brown, turning blackish with vertically grooved bark as they age. The distinctive, four-lobed leaves with a truncated tip measure up to 15 cm (6 in) long. They turn golden-yellow in autumn (3). The flowers, shaped like a tulip, are erect, up to 7 cm (2³/₄ in) across and generally open in June. The green sepals are differentiated or curled downwards; the creamy yellow petals have distinctive orange stripes at the base. There are about 30 stamens in the centre with long orange-yellow anthers. The fruits (samaras) are arranged in a cone-shaped collective fruit up to 5 cm

(2 in) long (4). They split when mature, leaving only the stem on the branch. Each samara with its stiff wing (5) measures about 5 mm ($^3/_{16}$ in) long and contains one or two seeds, which mature in October or November.

137

Tartar Honeysuckle
Lonicera tatarica

Caprifoliaceae

Honeysuckles are generally used to make untrimmed hedges, but can also be planted in large or small groups or as solitary specimens. They are quite undemanding woody plants, doing equally well in acid and alkaline soils. Unfortunately, when it is dry they are often infested by aphids. They tolerate shade and atmospheric pollution and are fully hardy in Britain. Bare-rooted plants are best planted in autumn. Older specimens need regular thinning out in early spring to encourage the growth of vigorous young shoots.

The species can be propagated from seeds in the autumn, or in spring after stratification. The commonest method is by hardwood cuttings taken in early winter. The low-growing cultivars can be propagated by softwood cuttings inserted in a propagator in June or July.

L. korolkowii is native to Central Asia. It is a shrub about 3 m (10 ft) high, producing masses of bluish white flowers in June. The light red berries ripen in autumn. The cultivar 'Aurora' bears pink flowers, larger than those of the species; 'Zabelii' has large, deep purple flowers.

L. maackii, a native of China, is a shrub up to 5 m (17 ft) high. The pleasantly scented white flowers open in June and age to yellow. The dark red berries remain on the branches long after the leaves have been shed.

The Tartar Honeysuckle is native to Southern Russia. It makes a wide-spreading shrub up to 3 m (10 ft) high. The young shoots (3) are grey-brown and hairless; the

2

138

ovate-lanceolate leaves measure 3—6 cm (1¹/₄—2¹/₄ in) long. The wide-open, salmon-pink flowers appear at the end of May and in June and are followed by carmine-red berries about 8 mm (⁵/₁₆ in) across, which ripen in early September.

Of the many cultivars in cultivation the following are most commonly grown: 'Alba', white flowers; 'Arnold Red', pink flowers, lush growth; 'Grandiflora', large, pure white flowers; 'Hack's Red' (1), white-pink flowers; 'Rosea' (2), large, pale pink flowers and 'Rubra', deep red flowers.

Box Thorn
Lycium barbarum
(syn. *L. halimifolium*)

Solanaceae

Box Thorns require plenty of space, so they are too large for small gardens. In parks and large landscape schemes they are used to anchor the soil on hillsides or in sand dunes and to form windbreaks. They are hardy pioneer plants for clothing waste land and to cover dumps and other infertile soils. On the other hand, Box Thorns soon grow wild, becoming troublesome weeds. Their densely tangled branches make them favourite nesting sites for song birds.

L. barbarum does well even in poor, sandy, salty and rather dry soils. It stands up well to a polluted atmosphere and the young shoots do not attract wild animals. Plant bare-rooted plants, preferably in autumn. Any plant that has become too large can be rejuvenated by cutting its branches hard back.

Box Thorns are easily propagated from hardwood cuttings in spring, by softwood cuttings in summer or by suckers and root cuttings in autumn.

The Chinese Box Thorn (*L. chinense*), grows wild in North-eastern China. Its somewhat rambling shoots up to 2 m (6½ ft) long are striped with grey-yellow and covered with sparse thorns. The large, ovate-lanceolate leaves are not shed until winter. The purple-violet flowers only about 1 cm (³/₈ in) across open in succession from June to October and are followed by elongated, ovate, orange-red berries about 25 mm (1 in) long.

Lycium barbarum (1), originally from China, has spread spontaneously to Europe, North Africa, Western Asia and eastern North America. It is a thick shrub with light grey shoots up to 3 m (10 ft) long (2). They are sparsely covered with thorns and grow erect when young, later arching down to the ground. Older branches are dull grey with the bark peeling off in threads. The narrow, lanceolate leaves are grey-green and about 6 cm (2¼ in) long. The lilac-purple flowers about 15 mm (⁵/₈ in) long are produced from June till autumn. They are long-stalked, with a greenish calyx and five-petalled

corolla. The elongated, oval scarlet-red
berries (3) up to 20 mm ($^{3}/_{4}$ in) long
ripen in September. Each berry contains
several yellowish, lentil-shaped
seeds.These fruits arc poisonous, so do
not plant Box Thorns where children are
likely to play.

2

1

3

Magnolia
Magnolia kobus
(syn. *M. tomentosa, M. gracilis*)

Magnoliaceae

Magnolias are among the most spectacular flowering woody plants. They are generally planted as single specimens in small gardens, but in parks and large gardens can also be planted in groups. This handsome tree needs plenty of space to spread freely and display its extraordinary beauty. Cut branchlets with developed buds will open indoors in a vase while it is still freezing and snowing outdoors.

Magnolias are happy in a warm sunny position and deep, humusrich, well aerated fertile soil, preferably slightly acid. They will not tolerate a polluted atmosphere. Container-grown plants with a well developed root ball are best planted in spring. It would be wise to protect the roots with a layer of peat or dry leaves before winter arrives, especially during the first two years after planting. Older plants are fully hardy in Britain. The species can be raised from stratified seeds in spring, but most magnolias are now propagated from cuttings inserted under plastic in July. One-year-old shoots layered in fairly moist, humusy soil will root within two years.

M. stellata is native to Central Japan. It is a slow-growing, thickly-branched shrub 2—3 m (6^1/$_2$—10 ft) high with ovate-lanceolate leaves up to 10 cm (4 in) long. It flowers in March before the leaves appear. The fragrant, star-shaped flowers are pinkish, later turning snow-white.

M. × *soulangiana*, most popular of all the magnolias, was produced by crossing *M. denudata* with *M. liliiflora*. It is a sparsely-branched, spreading tree up to 5 m (17 ft) high with obovate leaves. Its erect, bell-shaped white flowers suffused with pink open in April. Popular garden forms include: 'Alba Superba', early flowering with large snow-white flowers, and 'Alexandrina', white flowers, carmine outside.

Magnolia kobus, a native of Japan and Korea, makes a tree up to 10 m (33 ft) high, but in Britain it forms a much smaller shrub with obovate, shortly pointed leaves. The young shoots (2) are greyish brown, the buds covered with two felted scales. The creamy flowers (1) have a purple line on the outside of each petal and open before the leaves in April and May. The cylindrical, red collective fruits (3) with black-brown seeds (4) appear in autumn.

Mahonia, Oregon Grape
or Holly-leaved Berberis
Mahonia aquifolium   Berberidaceae

Mahonias are generally planted as groundcover or an underplanting beneath taller woody plants. They combine well with groups of conifers and can be planted together with other plants in large, portable garden containers. They also make good low hedges. The evergreen leaves are excellent for bouquets and wreaths.

M. aquifolium is an undemanding plant, doing equally well in sun and shade. It thrives in any garden soil including clay and sandy soils. *M. japonica*, on the other hand, needs a more sheltered position and a humus-rich, fertile, slightly acid soil.

Container-grown mahonias with a well developed root ball are best planted in the early spring. They stand up well to pruning, so cut them back to a suitable height immediately after flowering or in early spring. Unfortunately, mahonias can be hosts of the wheat or black stem rust. The Japanese and Chinese species need winter covering.

Specialist nurseries raise mahonias from mature seeds in autumn or after stratification in April. The cultivars are grafted on to potted rootstocks of *M. aquifolium*. You can also propagate them by layering.

M. japonica, an East Asian species, is smaller and more compact than *M. aquifolium*. The leaves, composed of 7—13 leaflets, are up to 40 cm (16 in) long, the pendulous racemes of flowers are lemon-yellow. The latter, opening from January to March, give off a pleasant scent of lilies-of-the-valley. The oval, bluish-black fruits are covered with bloom.

3

144

1

2

The Oregon Grape is an erect North American shrub about 1 m (3¹/₄ ft) high with yellow-brown twigs. The stiff, glossy, evergreen leaves (1) up to 20 cm (8 in) long are formed of 5—11 oval leaflets, which turn reddish in winter. The small, golden-yellow flowers (2) with a reddish tinge are borne in dense, upright racemes in March and April. The globular, purple-blue berries (3) with violet-red pulp and elongated seeds are covered with grey bloom and ripen in September.

Crab Apple
Malus hybrids

Rosaceae

Crab Apples make good-sized wide-spreading bushes or trees, so are best planted singly or in small groups. Compact forms look well planted in pots and as bonsai in special bowls. Their fruits are made into cider and jelly.

These trees are undemanding as regards soil and siting. A deep loamy soil enriched with humus in a slightly shaded position is best. Plant bare-rooted trees in autumn or spring. Plants that are well branched from the base need no pruning. Only prune sparsely-branched specimens to produce a thick and shapely head. Occasional thinning out is all that is necessary on older plants.

The species are propagated from stratified seeds sown in spring. Hybrids and cultivars are budded or grafted on to seedlings of *M. baccata* or *M. prunifolia*.

The Siberian Crab (*M. baccata*), is native to North-eastern Asia, where it grows up to 10 m (33 ft) high. It opens its white blossom in April. Its cherry-like fruits are yellow with a red spot.

M. floribunda, a Japanese species, makes a small tree 4—10 m (13—33 ft) high with a wide head. The pink flowers with white centres open in May. The fruits are yellow pomes.

M. prunifolia is native to Asia and is a shrub-like tree up to 5 m (17 ft) high. Its pure white flowers open in April. The elongated, oval fruits up to 3 cm (1¹/₄ in) long are yellowish-red.

1

3

Cultivars that lack the main features of the species are generally known as Malus hybrids (1, 2, 3). There are many of them and their correct botanical classification often poses a problem. Most widely grown are: 'Aldenhamensis' (*M.* × *purpurea*) with red leaves, semi-double, purple-red flowers and dark red fruits 2—3 cm ($^3/_4$—$1^1/_4$ in) long; 'Almey' (*M.* × *adstringens*), single, deep purple flowers with a lighter centre, globular fruits 2 cm ($^3/_4$ in) across, orange with a red spot; 'Charlottae' (*M. coronaria*), double, bluish-pink violet scented flowers, yellow-green fruits up to 4 cm ($1^1/_2$ in) across; 'Eleyi' (*M.* × *purpurea*), red leaves, single, wine red flowers and small, purple-red fruits; and 'Hillieri', deep red buds developing into semi-double, pale pink flowers and globular, yellow-orange fruits up to 2 cm ($^3/_4$ in) across.

Tree Peony, Moutan
Paeonia suffruticosa

Paeoniaceae

The woody species of peonies are remarkable for their lovely flowers. They look most attractive planted as solitary specimens in grass or among mat-forming perennials or creeping woody plants. They also look well planted in groups, especially in large gardens and parks. These peonies need a deep, humusy, well drained, slightly acid soil rich in nutrients. They flower best when planted in full sun, but also tolerate semi-shade. Plant them in September, while the soil is still warm, as the period of active growth begins very early in spring. Set grafts 5—8 cm (2—3¹/₄ in) beneath the soil so the cultivated part of the plant can develop its own roots. The first winter after planting it pays to cover the plant with a layer of processed bark, peat or dead leaves. Cut back flowered shoots so the plant cannot set seeds which weakens growth and results in poor flowering. Tree peonies resent root disturbance, so should be left in a permanent site. They are grafted on to the rootstock of *P. lactiflora* in late summer in a greenhouse. They are also propagated by stratified seeds sown in spring and germinated in heat under glass.

Besides *P. suffruticosa*, *P. delavayi* and *P. lutea* are sometimes seen in cultivation. *P. delavayi* makes a shrub up to 3 m (10 ft) high and flowers in June with rather small, saucer-shaped deep purple flowers. *P. lutea* is about 1 m (3¹/₄ ft) high and opens yellow flowers in May.

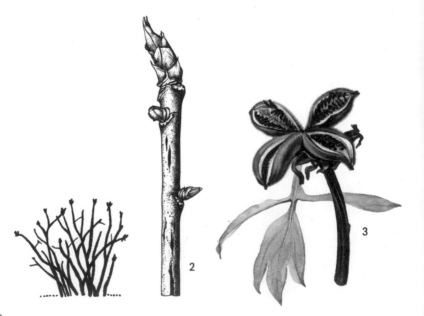

1

4

Paeonia suffruticosa (1, 2) is native to Tibet and North-western China, but even there it no longer grows in the wild. The first garden forms were bred in China and Japan centuries ago. French breeders introduced many cultivars in the second half of the 19th century. In its homeland, *P. suffruticosa* reaches a height of 2 m (6¹/₂ ft), but reaches only about half this size in Britain. The species flowers in late May and early June. Its semi-double,

pink-white flowers up to 15 cm (6 in) across have a violet spot rimmed with purple at the base of each petal. The fruits are bladders (3), splitting to reveal several large seeds (4). The species is no longer grown, having been superseded by a number of lovely cultivars with single, semi-double or double flowers. Their colours range from all shades of purple, carmine, red, salmon and pink to yellow and white.

149

Mock Orange
Philadelphus coronarius   Saxifragaceae

The genus *Philadelphus* contains some 70 species, originally distributed in Europe, Eastern Asia and North America. Mock Oranges are
rewarding shrubs, that look well planted as single specimens or in
large or small groups. They are used to cover areas of bare land on
modern housing estates and to fill in odd spaces, for they grow very
rapidly. If clipped into formal hedges they rarely produce flowers.

Mock Orange species do well in almost any garden soil, but the
cultivars require a more nourishing soil. All species are lime-loving.
They thrive in full sun, flowering less profusely and growing too tall
in shade. They stand up quite well to adverse city conditions and
their foliage does not attract browsing animals. Mock Oranges are
planted bare-rooted in autumn or early spring. Older specimens need
thinning out; cut back the oldest shoots just above the ground level
every two years to encourage new growth. Three to seven shoots are
enough to make a well branched shrub. Fast-growing species of
Mock Oranges are easily propagated from hardwood cuttings taken
in December or early spring and inserted in a garden bed. Slow-growing species can be propagated from softwood cuttings inserted under
plastic in a propagator in May or June.

Philadelphus coronarius (1) grows wild in an area extending from Northern Italy to the Caucasus. It is an erect shrub about 3 m (10 ft) high. The brown young shoots soon become hairless. Older branches are red-brown with peeling bark. The widely ovate leaves are up to 8 cm ($3^1/_4$ in) long. The racemes of creamy white, sweetly scented flowers are borne in June. The fruits mature in October and are oval to globular, four-valved capsules (2), splitting to reveal many small, elongated seeds (3).

Breeding has yielded many garden forms known as *P. coronarius* hybrids. These include 'Aureus', only about 1.5 m ($4^1/_2$ ft) high with small golden-yellow leaves aging to yellow-green and white flowers.

1

Philadelphus Virginalis hybrids
(syn. *P.* × *virginalis*)   Saxifragaceae

Philadelphus Virginalis hybrids were obtained by crossing P. Lemoinei hybrids with the cultivar *P. nivalis* 'Plenus' in the French nursery of Lemoine. They are displayed to best effect in groups, but also make good specimen shrubs for small gardens. Among the many interesting garden varieties commonly cultivated are 'Albatre', a shrub up to 2 m (6½ ft) high, flowering in July with very fragrant, semi-double pure white flowers up to 6 cm (2¼ in) across; 'Girandole', about 1.2 m (4 ft) high, with double, velvety white flowers about 3.5 cm (1¼ in) across that are scented and open in June; and 'Virginalis' itself, a profuse flowering shrub about 3 m (10 ft) high with richly fragrant, double, pure white flowers opening in June.

Philadelphus Lemoinei hybrids were produced in 1892 at the Lemoine nursery by crossing *P. coronarius* and *P. microphyllus.* The original hybrids gave rise to many cultivars such as 'Avalanche', up to 2 m (6½ ft) high, with very fragrant, single, milk-white flowers opening in early July; 'Erectus', about 2 m (6½ ft) high, with very fragrant, single, pure white blossoms up to 3 cm (1¼ in) across; 'Manteau d'Hermine', a thickly-branched shrub only 1 m (3¼ ft) high, with faintly fragrant, double, snow-white flowers borne in June, and 'Mont Blanc' of upright habit, with single, white, very fragrant flowers up to 3 cm (1¼ in) across.

Philadelphus Purpureo-maculatus hybrids, syn. *P.* × *purpureo-maculatus,* are shrubs only 1.5 m (5 ft) high, also bred in France. The dainty, black-grey shoots soon become hairless. The widely oval leaves up to 3.5 cm (1¼ in) long are sparsely covered with hairs on the underside. They flower during June and July with very fragrant, single, white blossoms flushed purple-red at the base.

Philadelphus Virginalis hybrids (1) are erect shrubs about 2.5 m (8½ ft) high. Their shoots are covered with hairs but these are soon shed. Older branches are brown with peeling bark. The ovate leaves up to 7 cm (2¾ in) long are felted beneath. The dense racemes of sweetly scented, white flowers are borne in June.

P. Lemoinei hybrids are of a more
compact habit. Their oval leaves are
only about 1.5 cm ($^5/_8$ in) long; the
white flowers are borne singly or in
clusters of three during June and July.

1

153

Ninebark
Physocarpus opulifolius
(syn. *Spiraea opulifolia*)

Rosaceae

Ninebarks are ornamental shrubs not yet as widely grown as they deserve. They are suitable for masking eyesores in the garden and filling spaces among taller woody plants. They look well grouped in parks and gardens and are also used to make unclipped or formal hedges and to anchor soil on crumbly hillsides. They make delightful shrubs for children's playgrounds, for their bladder-like fruits make a popping noise when squeezed.

Ninebarks are undemanding shrubs that tolerate semishade and polluted city conditions. They may be damaged by severe black frosts, but after being cut back rapidly grow again. Bare-rooted plants can be planted in autumn or early spring. Old shrubs are rejuvenated by thinning out congested growth. Nurseries propagate physocarpus from seeds sown in heated frames in autumn or by cuttings inserted in a garden bed in spring.

P. amurensis came originally from North-eastern China and Korea. It is a shrub about 2 m (6¹/₂ ft) high, of erect habit when young, but tending to become somewhat pendulous when mature. The young shoots are covered with grey hairs, but these soon disappear. The leaves are three to five-lobed and up to 10 cm (4 in) across. The white flowers open in June.

Physocarpus opulifolius (1) is native to eastern North America, where it grows on river banks and rocky slopes. It makes a twiggy shrub up to 3 m (10 ft) high with somewhat arching branches. The light brown young shoots are vertically wrinkled and broom-like. Older branches are brown with the bark peeling off in vertical strips (2). The leaves are five-lobed, about 9 cm (3¹/₂ in) across and turn red in autumn. The flowers, arranged in hemispherical umbels, open in June. They measure

3

154

about 1 cm ($^3/_8$ in) across and are white
with reddish anthers. The fruits are
inflated, reddish bladders (3), which
make a loud cracking sound when
crushed between the fingers. They
contain yellowish seeds and remain on
the shrub far into the winter. The
cultivar 'Lutea' puts out yellow leaves,
which later turn bronze-green. It grows
slower than the species and reaches
a maximum height of 2 m ($6^1/_2$ ft).

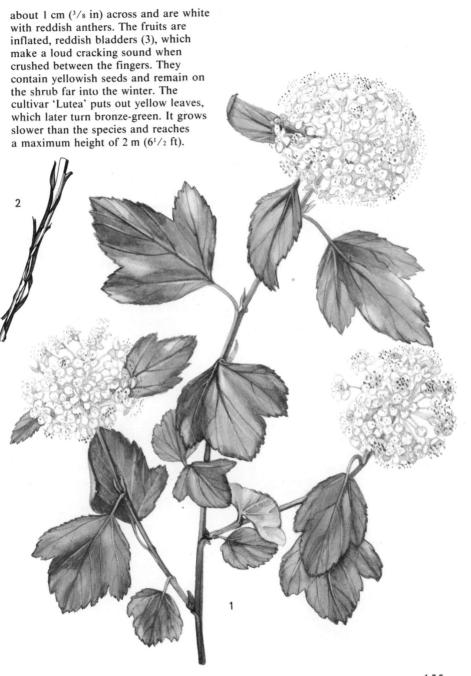

155

Shrubby Cinquefoil
Potentilla fruticosa

Rosaceae

Potentillas are useful shrubs, which serve a variety of purposes. They look well planted singly in a bed of perennials or on a rock garden and are displayed to good effect in loose groupings in front of taller shrubs. They stand up well to pruning, so are sometimes used to make uncut or clipped low hedges. They have recently been used as groundcover plants too.

Shrubby Cinquefoils need full sun, as they flower poorly in shade. They tolerate a fairly dry soil and are fully hardy in Britain. Plant them while they are dormant, preferably in the autumn or early spring. Container-grown plants can be planted from spring to autumn. Older specimens usually lose the leaves on old branches at ground level, so cut old growth hard back now and then and give the shrubs a feed in early spring to keep them bushy. Even old plants tolerate transplanting.

The species can be propagated from seeds sown immediately after harvesting, but they are often propagated from softwood cuttings in May and June. They can also be propagated from suckers. When the lowest buds have rooted, detach the shoots and plant them in a sunny position. The species itself is no longer cultivated, having been replaced by many cultivars of varying size and habit.

The Shrubby Cinquefoil (1) is distributed throughout most of the Northern Hemisphere, growing wild in the lowlands and on mountain slopes. It is a densely-branched, deciduous shrub about 1 m (3¹/₄ ft) high. Its young shoots (2) are yellow-brown, the bark of older branches peels off. The leaves are formed of three to seven lanceolate-elliptic leaflets covered with fine hairs on both sides. It bears a profusion of creamy-yellow flowers from May to September. The collective fruit (3), ripening in September, is formed of dry achenes (4) containing oval seeds.

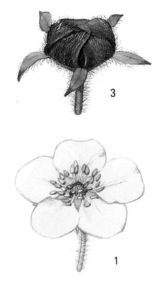

156

The most widely grown cultivars are: 'Abbotswood', 90 cm (3 ft) high, with greyish leaves and pure white flowers; 'Goldfinger', bushy, 75 cm (30 in) high with deep yellow flowers; 'Princess', robust, 75 cm (30 in) high, flowering May to early November, pink flowers 3 cm (1 1/4 in) across, 'Red Ace', low-growing, 50—75 cm (20—30 in) high, spreading 100—120 cm (3 1/4—4 ft), bright vermilion flame flowers; 'Jackman's Variety', up to 1.5 m (5 ft) high, golden-yellow flowers up to 4 cm (1 1/2 in) across, and 'Klondike', of low compact habit, with deep yellow flowers.

157

Cherry Laurel
Prunus laurocerasus

Rosaceae

The Cherry Laurel is native to the Balkans and Turkey, but has become naturalized throughout Southern and Western Europe. It needs a shaded position, so this evergreen shrub is often planted under taller woody plants. If planted in movable tubs, always site them in a shady place and overwinter them in a cool greenhouse if weather is severe. Cherry Laurels also make good clipped or unclipped hedges.

Being an evergreen species, Cherry Laurel is more demanding as regards soil and location than other species of *Prunus*. It is best planted on a north aspect in front of buildings to give them the necessary shade. The small-leaved Balkan varieties and their cultivars are much hardier than the large-leaved forms from the Caucasus, which can be damaged by black frosts. If they are, cut them hard back to stimulate rapid growth. Cherry Laurels generally thrive in a humus-rich, fairly moist soil. They do not tolerate limy soils, but stand up well to atmospheric pollution in industrial areas.

Plant Cherry Laurels with an intact root ball. The best time for planting is spring. Give the plants winter protection for the first few years after planting to stop the soil getting frost-bound too deep and to protect the shrubs from winter and early spring sunshine.

In its homeland, the Cherry Laurel (1) makes a tree or shrub up to 6 m (20 ft) high, but reaches a maximum of 2 m (6½ ft) in Britain. The young shoots (2) are green and hairless, the ovate-lanceolate leaves are leathery and up to 15 cm (6 in) long. The small, creamy white flowers are arranged in upright racemes up to 12 cm (4¾ in) long. They open in May, but sometimes there is a second flowering in the autumn. The flowers are followed by black-red oval fruits up to 12 mm (½ in) long (3).

The cultivar 'Caucasica' is upright-growing and hardy, with leaves up to 15 cm (6 in) long; 'Herbergii', hardy, conical habit, laurel-like leaves; 'Otto Luyken', a dense, wide-spreading shrub barely 1 m (3¼ ft) high with narrow leaves; 'Schipkaensis', fully hardy, up to 2 m (6½ ft) high, with

1

158

1

narrow leaves; and 'Zabeliana',
lower-growing, horizontally branching,
fully hardy, with narrow, willow-like
leaves.

CAUTION: All parts of this plant are
extremely poisonous, as they contain
hydrogen cyanide.

3

2

Blackthorn, Sloe
Prunus spinosa

Rosaceae

The genus *Prunus* contains some 200 species growing in the temperate zone of the Northern Hemisphere. Besides ornamentals, it includes fruit trees such as apricots, peaches, greengages, plums and cherries. Species grown for their flowers are planted singly or in small groups in front of taller woody plants. The early-flowering species can be forced. Their flowering sprigs make delightful home decorations. The edible fruits of *P. spinosa* — sloes — are used to make homemade wine. All species introduced (see the following two pages) are quite undemanding as regards soil. They are happy in sunny or sheltered situations and do not mind a polluted atmosphere.

The deciduous species are planted bare-rooted in the autumn or early spring. Prune the shoots to a desirable shape. After this, removing diseased and damaged growth is all that is required. The species are raised from seeds sown in the autumn or after stratification in March. Hybrids and cultivars are grafted in a greenhouse in winter or budded on to rootstocks of related species in summer.

P. cerasifera is an erect, daintily-branched shrub with sparse thorns. It is native to the Caucasus and Turkey, where it grows up to 6 m (20 ft) high. Its white flowers with pinkish centres open as early as March. The cultivar 'Atropurpurea' ('Pissardii') has red-brown leaves and pink-white flowers. 'Nigra' has black-red foliage with lilac-pink blossom in April.

Blackthorn (1) is distributed across most of Europe, North Africa and Turkey, growing mostly in wine-growing areas. It is a spindly, thickly-branched shrub about 3 m (10 ft) high, forming a thicket of underground suckers. Its red-brown shoots (2) are covered with grey hairs; older branches are black. The elliptic-lanceolate leaves are about 4 cm (1¹/₂ in) long. Its white flowers up to 15 mm (⁵/₈ in) across appear before the leaves in April. The globular fruits (sloes —3, stone — 4) are blue-black with a grey bloom and ripen in autumn. They have an astringent taste and cannot be eaten before the first autumn frosts. They are widely used in popular medicine and pharmacy. Blackthorn thickets attract nesting birds and the flowers are much visited by bees. The cultivar 'Plena' has double, white flowers, while 'Purpurea' displays blood red leaves and pinkish blossom.

4

1

2

3

161

Prunus triloba is a handsome shrub, producing a profusion of small flowers in early spring. Winter protection of foliage and green brushwood is a must in harsh climatic conditions.

The Peach, *P. persica*, is a native of China, of which there are many fruiting varieties. The cultivar 'Clara Meyer' is grown for its ornamental blossom, being particularly suitable for viniferous regions. Its double, pink-red flowers about 4 cm (1½ in) across are borne in April.

The Dwarf Russian Almond (*P. tenella*), is distributed from the Mediterranean area to Eastern Siberia, growing in lowlands and also on mountain slopes. It is a twiggy, wide-spreading shrub about 1 m (3¼ ft) high, that produces many suckers. The hairless, olive-green shoots have prominent lenticels; older branches are flushed with silver-grey. The leaves are up to 7 cm (2¾ in) long, narrowly elliptic or obovate with pointed tips. They appear in May at the same time as the pink, sessile flowers up to 3 cm (1¼ in) across. They are borne in axillary clusters along the shoots. The fruits are yellow-grey, hairy and rather dry drupes containing an unwrinkled, oval stone with a rough surface. As a dwarf this species is suitable for growing in large pots and troughs. It can also be forced to produce flowering sprigs as early as late winter. The cultivar 'Alba' has pure white flowers, but 'Firehill' is pinkish crimson.

Prunus triloba (1) grows wild on mountain slopes in the Chinese provinces of Hupei and Shantung. It is a wide-spreading densely branched shrub up to 2 m (6½ ft) high. The shoots are dark brown; the bark of old branches is black-brown and peels. The widely elliptic leaves (2) are mostly three-lobed and up to 8 cm (3¼ in) long. The sessile, pink flowers are borne

1

along the whole length of the previous
year's shoots, appearing before the
leaves as early as late March and April.
The fruits are globular, finely hairy, red
drupes. The cultivar 'Plena' with double,
pink flowers like small roses does not
bear fruit. *P. triloba* var. *simplex* is
a shrub about 3 m (10 ft) high with dark
brown, hairless shoots and grey-brown
older branches. Its single, pink flowers
soon wilt and fall.

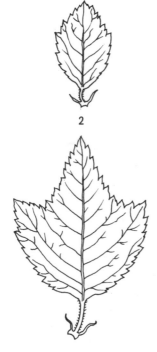

2

1

163

Hop Tree
Ptelea trifoliata
Rutaceae

Hop Trees are among those shrubs used chiefly to fill spaces among taller trees in landscaping schemes. But they do make good specimen shrubs for a small garden, where they should be planted where the fruits can be seen at close quarters. Fruit-bearing twigs can be cut and put in a vase for home decoration in the autumn.

Hop Trees are undemanding shrubs that grow well even in fairly dry, poor soils, though they prefer moist sites. They tolerate polluted atmospheres and thrive in full sun as well as partial shade. They may be damaged by severe black frosts. The whole plant gives off an unpleasant smell, which repels wild animals.

Plant bare-rooted shrubs in autumn or early spring. Container-grown specimens can be planted at any time of year, preferably from spring to autumn. Cut them hard back to get good branching and remove dead growth in spring. They need no winter protection in Britain.

The species is propagated from seeds, which are sown when they have matured, or stratified and sown in spring. The rarer species and cultivars are grafted on to *P. trifoliata* rootstock in greenhouses in winter or directly in the garden in early spring.

The Hop Tree is a sparsely-branched shrub up to 5 m (17 ft) high, which originated in North America, where its range extends from Ontario to Florida. The red-brown, glossy young shoots later become yellow-brown with glandular spots. The bark gives off a bitter smell like hops. The trifoliate, long-petioled leaves (1) are formed of ovate-lanceolate leaflets up to 10 cm (4 in) long with translucent dots. The greenish white, fragrant flowers are arranged in cymose heads (2) and open from late May to July. The fruits are flat, non-dehiscent, orbicular samaras about 2 cm (³/₄ in) long, and have broad wings and prominent veins (3). Each samara contains two seeds. The fruits mature in September and remain on the branches until late winter.

Widely grown cultivars are 'Aurea', with golden-yellow leaves, and 'Fastigiata' of erect, columnar habit.

165

Firethorn
Pyracantha coccinea

Rosaceae

Firethorns are most attractive as isolated specimens, but are also planted in small groups or as an underplanting beneath tall trees. They stand up well to pruning and so can be used for trimmed as well as· uncut hedges. They look very effective set against walls and trellises and can be used to cover and anchor crumbly hillsides.

Pyracanthas have no special requirements as regards soil and siting, though they do best on a nourishing, fairly dry soil, preferably supplied with lime. For a good crop of flowers and rich-coloured fruits be sure to choose a sunny position, though pyracanthas usually do well even in partial shade. Their foliage is attractive to browsing animals. These shrubs are not fully hardy in harsh conditions and can suffer frost damage, but they rapidly grow again after being cut back.

Plant Firethorns with an intact root ball. Planting is best done in early spring so that their roots can spread freely before the onset of winter. Cut them hard back after planting to reduce transpiration and encourage good branching. Mature plants will not tolerate transplanting.

Pyracanthas can be propagated from seed, but this method is not widely used, as the seedlings vary in their characteristics, often being less hardy and producing fewer fruits than plants raised from softwood cuttings. The cuttings are best taken in June and inserted under plastic in a mist propagation unit. Well ripened cuttings can also be taken in the autumn and rooted in a cool greenhouse.

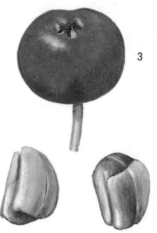

3

166

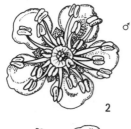

2

1

The Firethorn (1) is an evergreen shrub about 3 m (10 ft) high, originally from Southern Europe and Turkey. The oval to lanceolate leaves are 2—4 cm ($^3/_4$—$1^1/_2$ in) long. Corymbs of creamy white flowers (2) appear in May and June. The collective fruit is composed of globular, orange-red pomes and remain on the branches far into the winter.

The species is no longer in cultivation. Best known garden forms include: 'Lalandei', a spreading shrub with orange-red berries up to 10 mm ($^3/_8$ in) long and 'Praecox', only 1 m ($3^1/_4$ ft) high, with dense thorns and scarlet-red fruits. Other garden forms are known collectively as Pyracantha hybrids and bear yellow, orange or red fruits.

167

Common Buckthorn
Rhamnus cathartica

Rhamnaceae

Groups of buckthorns are often planted in landscaped areas. Common Buckthorn is a pioneer shrub that rapidly covers dry slopes, scree and waste land. It can also make thick hedges.

Common Buckthorn needs a fairly dry, open-textured soil and is a lime-lover. The Alder Buckthorn (see below), on the other hand, prefers moist, humus-rich and even slightly acid soils. Both species will tolerate a polluted environment and are fully hardy in Britain. They are best planted while leafless, in spring or autumn. The only pruning necessary is the removal of any dead branches. Nurseries propagate both species from stratified seeds in spring. Other species of thorny Buckthorns are grafted on to seedlings of *R. cathartica*, thornless ones on to *R. frangula*.

The Alder Buckthorn (*R. frangula*), forms part of the undergrowth of humid woods across most of Europe, Western Asia and North Africa and has also been introduced to North America. It is a thornless shrub about 3 m (10 ft) high. The felted shoots turn grey-brown with light lenticels when mature. Clusters of up to 20 greenish flowers appear in May and June, followed by glossy, violet-black drupes.

Common Buckthorn (1) grows wild on sunny, limy slopes in Europe and North-west Asia. It is an irregularly-branched shrub about 4 m (13 ft) high. The grey young shoots are armed with terminal thorns; the bark of

168

older branches turns almost black and peels off in horizontal strips. The orbicular-ovate leaves are up to 6 cm (2¹/₄ in) long. The small, greenish-white flowers are very fragrant and appear during May and June. The fruits mature in late September. They are green globular drupes aging to black (2) and contain four triangular stones (3) fused at the base. The hard dense wood with glossy red-brown heart is valued for wood turning. The bark has been used since ancient times to make dyes.

CAUTION: Unripe fruits, leaves and bark contain emodin, a glycoside causing retching, nausea and other problems, so Common Buckthorn is best not planted where children play.

Rhododendron, Azalea
Rhododendron luteum
(syn. *Azalea pontica*)

Ericaceae

Deciduous azaleas have become popular ornamental shrubs over the many years they have been grown. First the wild species were transplanted to our gardens. Later, some were deliberately crossed to obtain early-flowering hardy offspring with more attractive flowers than those of the original species. Nowadays azaleas are planted in rock and heath gardens, ornamental beds and large containers, for their striking beauty can be used to good effect almost anywhere.

Deciduous azaleas grow best in a fairly warm moist position and a well drained soil containing little or no lime, the optimum pH value being 4—4.5. Partial shade suits them best, but they can be grown in full sun, provided they are given plenty of water. Container-grown plants are planted with intact root balls. The roots need plenty of air, so plant this shrub only 3—5 cm (1¹/₄—2 in) under the soil surface. Soak the plant in a bucket of water for about an hour before planting to make sure its root ball is well moistened. Azaleas are best protected from frost with a layer of peat or bark chippings for the first couple of years after planting out. No pruning is necessary.

The species are raised from seeds sown in heated frames in May or in winter in a greenhouse. Cultivars are increased from cuttings taken from July to November. Poor-rooting kinds are best grafted on to seedlings of the species. Grafting is best done in a greenhouse in January or February or in a heated frame from May to July.

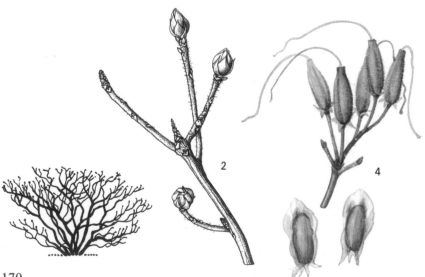

Rhododendron luteum (1) is native to Eastern Europe, Turkey and the Caucasus. It is a rather sparsely-branched shrub up to 2 m (6½ ft) high. The young shoots (2) are clothed with hairs. The sparsely hairy, lanceolate leaves (3) 6—12 cm (2¼—3¾ in) long turn purple-red in autumn. The deep yellow, funnel-shaped flowers 3—5 cm (1¼—2 in) across are very fragrant and appear before the leaves in May. The fruit is a cylindrical woody capsule (4) containing fine seeds. It ripens in September.

R. luteum is one of the parents of the well-known Ghent Azaleas, bearing a wealth of flowers in different shades of yellow, pink and red. Crosses between *R. luteum* and other species yielded many other groups of cultivars such as Knap Hill, Exbury, Mollis, Occidentale and Rustica. All produce a profusion of lovely flowers in a variety of colours.

Rhodotypos
Rhodotypos scandens

Rosaceae

Rhodotypos scandens has not been widely grown yet, which is a pity as it makes a handsome shrub for landscaping as well as in parks and gardens. It is best planted in small mixed groups under taller shrubs, but can also be used to fill odd spaces or make untrimmed hedges.

Rhodotypos have no special requirements, growing well in both dry and moist soils. They can adapt well even to poor, sandy soils. Lack of sun results in poor flowering, though rhodotypos can stand full sun as well as shade. Plant bare-rooted leafless shrubs in autumn or spring. Cut back the shoots to ensure good branching. Later thin out old wood occasionally to encourage new growth. Overgrown neglected plants should be cut back close to ground level. Rhodotypos can be damaged by frost in exposed places but they will soon make new growth after being cut back.

Specialist nurseries propagate Rhodotypos from seeds, of which it produces sufficient. They germinate well and can be sown in autumn or after stratification in spring. The quickest method of propagation is by softwood cuttings, as hardwood ones are slow to root.

Rhodotypos scandens (1) originally grew in Japan and China, but plants that have escaped from cultivation grow wild across most of Europe. In its homeland it is a wide-spreading shrub up to 5 m (17 ft) high, but in Britain it barely reaches 1.5 m (5 ft). The young shoots are olive-brown, the older branches brownish. The opposite leaves are up to 10 cm (4 in) long, with a wrinkled surface reminiscent of those of *Kerria japonica*. The four-part flowers up to

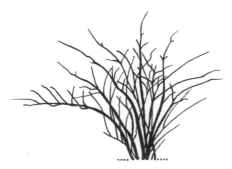

3

5 cm (2 in) across have white petals
surrounding numerous stamens. They
are produced in May and June and are
followed by shiny black, dry, pea-sized
fruits (2) containing large blackish
brown seeds (3). The fruits are borne in
fours on a single calyx with large dry
sepals and remain on the shrub till the
following spring.

Stagshorn Sumach
Rhus typhina

Anacardiaceae

Stagshorn Sumachs rank high among popular foliage shrubs. When planted in grass or among mat-forming perennials, they make most decorative and spectacular specimens in gardens. They can also be planted in small groups in parks and are displayed to good effect planted in large pots stood in streets and other open spaces.

Stagshorn Sumachs have no special requirements as regards soil. They are happy even in a rather poor, very dry soil. Give them a sunny position for the leaves to develop a rich coloration. These plants stand up quite well to the smoke-filled environment of cities and industrial regions and are fully hardy in Britain.

Bare-rooted plants should be planted only during autumn or early spring while dormant. Container-grown specimens can be planted at any time during the growing season. No regular pruning is required, only remove dead or damaged branches from older shrubs. Stagshorn Sumachs spread rapidly by suckering and can become rather troublesome, especially in a small garden. Specialist nurseries propagate Staghorn Sumachs from seed in spring. Vegetative propagation by suckers is also very easy. Garden forms can be propagated from heeled cuttings taken in February or March and inserted in a heated frame or propagator.

Stagshorn Sumachs are unisexual plants with male and female flowers on separate trees, so to obtain fruits plant both male and female bushes.

Rhus typhina is native to the limy slopes of eastern North America. It has become naturalized almost throughout Europe, where it has been cultivated for

centuries. It is a fast-growing, wide-spreading shrub or tree with many trunks reaching a height of 5 m (17 ft). The thick, grey-brown shoots are clothed with rusty-brown hairs. Older branches are dark brown. The alternate leaves up to 40 cm (16 in) long are formed of 11—31 lanceolate leaflets which exude a milky-white juice. They turn a magnificent orange-red in autumn before they fall. The tiny yellow-green flowers are borne in dense, upright panicles (1) in June. The fruits are dark red, glandular hairy nuts about 4 mm ($^1/_8$ in) in diameter. They are borne in flame-shaped collective fruits (2, 3), which remain on the branches throughout the winter. The cultivar 'Laciniata' has finely-dissected, feathery leaves.

1

2

3

Mountain Currant
Ribes alpinum

Saxifragaceae

The genus *Ribes* comprises some 150 species, distributed in the cold and temperate zones of the Northern Hemisphere and less widely in South America. Currants are mostly planted in groups and are used to cover areas of bare land and slopes and to fill odd spaces. Low-growing species and cultivars look well planted in a rock garden or in large tubs and other containers. They also make good clipped and un-cut hedges. Currants have no special requirements, adapting well to almost all soil, climatic and light conditions. They thrive in loamy, sandy and gravel soils (acid or alkaline), provided they are given enough moisture. They stand up well to atmospheric pollution. Most prefer a sunny site, only *R. alpinum* and *R. aureum* do well in partial shade.

Bare-rooted plants should be planted while leafless in autumn or spring. Cut back old shoots after flowering to stimulate new growth. Overgrown neglected specimens can be rejuvenated by cutting them hard back.

Currants are readily propagated from hardwood cuttings in September or June. Slow-growing species and cultivars are best propagated from softwood cuttings inserted in a propagator in June and July. Species that root poorly should be grafted on to *R. aureum* root-stocks in March. Species that produce underground shoots can be propagated from suckers. *R. sanguineum* (see p. 178) and its cultivars are propagated from one-year-old layers.

2

5

The Mountain Currant (1) is distributed
from European forests to Eastern
Siberia, its natural range extending to
North-west Africa. It is a thickly-
branched shrub up to 1.8 m (6 ft) high
with yellow-brown young shoots (2),
black-grey branches and peeling bark.
The three-lobed leaves measure 3—5 cm
($1^1/_4$—2 in) across and are covered with
sparse hairs. The five-part yellow-green
flowers open in May. The male flowers
(3) are arranged in clusters of 10—30,
while the females (4) have smaller sepals
and are borne two to five to each
upright raceme. After being pollinated
and fertilized, the female flowers
develop into red berries (5) about 6 mm
($^1/_4$ in) across. They have a dull taste
and contain plenty of yellow-brown
seeds (6).

The cultivar 'Pumilum' is rarely higher
then 1 m ($3^1/_4$ ft).

3

4

6

1

Red Flowering Currant
Ribes sanguineum

Saxifragaceae

The Flowering Currant is a widely-cultivated and rewarding ornamental shrub. It stands up well to regular pruning, so is commonly
used to make both clipped and informal hedges.

R. americanum, a native of North American forests, is a shrub up to
2 m (6$^1/_2$ ft) high. Its brown branches arch down to the ground. The
three-lobed leaves up to 8 cm (3$^1/_4$ in) long turn scarlet-brown in autumn. The drooping racemes of green-yellow flowers appear from
April to May and are followed by black berries with green pulp that
mature in July.

The Golden Currant (*R. aureum*) is native to the mountain slopes
of North America. It is a lush-growing shrub about 2.5 m (8$^1/_2$ ft)
high. Its yellow-brown shoots are covered with fine hairs; older
branches are black-brown with the bark peeling off in strips. The
three-lobed leaves up to 5 cm (2 in) across turn red in autumn. The
golden-yellow flowers are flushed red and are scented of carnations.
They are arranged in drooping racemes and appear from April to
May. They are followed by black-brown berries, which are made into
jelly or left on the branches for birds.

R. multiflorum originated on the mountain slopes of central Italy
and Sardinia, where it grows 2 m (6$^1/_2$ ft) high. It has pale brown
shoots and ash grey branches that carry cordate, three- to five-lobed
leaves felted grey-white beneath. The drooping inflorescence is up to
12 cm (4$^3/_4$ in) long. The dark red berries are edible.

The Flowering Currant (1) came from
the mountain slopes of North America.
It is an erect shrub about 2.5 m (8$^1/_2$ ft)
high. The red-green, finely hairy shoots
(2) later turn into grey-brown branches
with peeling bark. The three- to

3

1

2

five-lobed leaves measure up to 10 cm (4 in) long with prominent veins and white-felted undersides. The drooping racemes of pink flowers are up to 8 cm (3¹/₄ in) long and appear on the bare wood in late April. The fruits are persistent black berries with a blue-white bloom. Widely-grown cultivars include: 'Atrorubens', with profuse, small, blood-red flowers in short racemes; 'King Edward VII' (3), of compact habit, with large red flowers; and 'Pulborough Scarlet' with deep red flowers.

179

Rose Acacia
Robinia hispida

Fabaceae

Robinias are mostly trees and only a few like *Robinia hispida* are shrubs. This makes a choice specimen shrub suitable even for a small garden. As it is not very tall, the Rose Acacia can be planted in a rock or heath garden or in a large tub.

Robinias require plenty of sun. They will succeed even in poor, dry, stony soils with a considerable lime and salt content. They tolerate atmospheric pollution. Although they are almost fully hardy in Britain, they prefer a sheltered position, as their brittle branches are easily damaged by wind. Plant them bare-rooted in autumn or early spring while they are leafless. No regular pruning is necessary. Rootstocks of grafted specimens sometimes produce lateral offshoots. Cut these back promptly to stop the shrub becoming exhausted.

Rose Acacia is propagated by grafting on to *R. pseudoacacia* (False Acacia) rootstock between February and April. The scions can be grafted at ground level or on to the crown. Propagation by suckers or heeled cuttings is also possible. The *R. pseudoacacia* rootstock is usually increased from seed stored in a dry place during the winter, then sown outdoors in April or May.

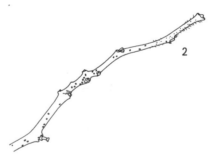

Robinia hispida (1) occurs widely on mountain slopes in the South-eastern United States. It is a thornless, sparsely-branched shrub with brittle wood, that grows to a height of 2 m (6½ ft). The olive-brown shoots (2) are covered with long dense red hairs; older branches are red-brown and susceptible to wind damage. The leaves (3) are composed of 7—17 widely elliptic leaflets some 5 cm (2 in) long. The shrub blooms in May with sometimes a repeat flowering in September. The large, purple-pink flowers are arranged in 2- to 6-flowered, hairy, drooping racemes. Unfortunately this species is not fragrant. The cultivar 'Macrophylla' makes lusher growth than the species. Its twigs are almost hairless and not so brittle. The flowers appear about two weeks earlier than in the species.

CAUTION: The bark and roots contain a poisonous chemical, so this shrub should not be planted where children play.

Dog Rose
Rosa canina

Rosaceae

The Dog Rose is a suitable subject for a big garden, as it requires ample space to develop its spreading habit. It is most suitable for untrimmed hedges, but also makes a good pioneer plant used mostly to cover slopes and provide shelter for birds. In rose nurseries it is used as a rootstock for budding ornamental roses.

The Dog Rose will grow even in rather poor, dry and stony soils. It is a lime-loving plant, which does best in deep, fertile, well drained soils with a pH value of 5.5—6.5. It will tolerate a smoky environment. A sunny site is desirable, as it does not flower so profusely in partial shade. Plant leafless bare-rooted plants in late October in well cultivated soil enriched with compost. Remove only frost-damaged branches in spring. No winter protection is necessary. Rejuvenate old shrubs by hard pruning.

This shrub is easy to propagate from its plentiful suckers. Nurseries sometimes propagate Dog Roses from selected seeds to obtain more rootstocks. The seeds are stratified for a year then sown outdoors in autumn or spring. It can also be propagated from cuttings, taken in March and April or from June to July and inserted in a propagator or heated frame.

The Dog Rose (1), a Eurasian species, is familiar as a native of our hillsides and forest margins. It is a wide-spreading shrub some 2 m (6½ ft) high with somewhat twisted green shoots (2).

Older branches are olive-brown with sparse, hooked thorns, which are easy to peel off. The alternately-arranged leaves are formed of 5—7 elliptic leaflets with two stipules at the base of each leaf

3

stalk and are up to 12 cm (4³/₄ in) long.
The sweetly-scented flowers are borne
singly or in twos and threes at the tips
of branches. They are white to pink and
open in early June. The scarlet-red rose
hips are elliptic or bottle-shaped with
yellowish brown hairy achenes inside
(3). They mature in October. Being
a rich source of vitamin C, the hips are
used to make teas, wines and preserves.

183

Austrian Briar
Rosa foetida
(syn. *R. lutea*)

Rosaceae

The Austrian Briar is native to an area extending from Turkey to the North-western Himalayas, but it has gradually become naturalized throughout Europe. It is a rather hardy and rapidly-growing woody plant, used to good effect in gardens as a single specimen or planted in groups in parks. The same is true of the following species of ornamental garden roses:

Père Hugo's Rose (*R. hugonis*), is a native of Central China, a shrub with arching branches reaching about 2.5 m (8¹/₂ ft) high. The light yellow flowers up to 5 cm (2 in) across are borne on sideshoots along its branches in May and June.

The Mount Omei Rose (*R. omeiensis*) is a shrub 3—4 m (10—13 ft) high, which originated in the Chinese province of Szechwan. It flowers in May and June with white flowers some 3 cm (1¹/₄ in) across.

The Scotch or Burnet Rose (*R. pimpinellifolia*, syn. *R. spinosissima*), grows wild in the sand dunes of Europe and Asia. Reaching a maximum height of 1 m (3¹/₄ ft), it spreads by underground shoots to cover large areas of land. Its white flowers flushed with yellow or pink measure about 5 cm (2 in) across. They open in May and June. This species has many most decorative garden forms such as 'Frühlingsgold' with single, golden-yellow flowers, and 'Frühlingszauber' with semi-double, light red flowers.

R. xanthina is distributed throughout Northern China, Mongolia, Central Asia and Korea. It is a shrub about 2 m (6¹/₂ ft) high, with arching branches bearing semi-double, golden-yellow flowers about 4 cm (1¹/₂ in) across.

3

Rosa foetida (1) reaches a height of 3 m (10 ft) in Britain. Its arching branches and thin, shiny brown twigs are covered with thick, straight prickles bristly at the base. The compound leaves (2) are composed of 5—9 leaflets about 2.5 cm (1 in) long. The single, yellow flowers about 5 cm (2 in) across have an unpleasant scent. They open in June and are followed by the small, red hips, which only occasionally mature in Britain.

The cultivar 'Bicolor' (3) is a slow-growing shrub about 1.5 m (5 ft) high. Its yellow flowers with orange-red centres are up to 6 cm ($2^1/_4$ in) wide. 'Persian Yellow' was brought from Persia in 1838. It is about 1.5 m (5 ft) high and bears small, double, golden-yellow flowers in early June.

Ramanas Rose
Rosa rugosa
Rosaceae

Rosa rugosa is mainly grown as a hedging plant, but is also used for street borders or planted in large groups in parks. It will even tolerate the salt spread on city streets in winter. It is a valuable nectar-producing plant too.

Rosa rugosa thrives even in poor, dry sandy soils which are acid. It withstands atmospheric pollution and is fully hardy in Britain. Hardwood cuttings should be taken in December, then inserted in a garden bed in March or April. This plant can also be propagated by suckers, which are produced in great numbers, and from stratified seeds in spring.

Many Rugosa cultivars with attractive flowers are offered. They include: 'Conrad Ferdinand Mayer', up to 2.5 m (8½ ft) high, double pink flowers tinted silver, measuring up to 12 cm (4¾ in) across, sweetly-scented, flowering in June; 'Dr. Eckener', a somewhat tender shrub up to 2.5 m (8½ ft) high, fragrant, double coppery-pink to golden-yellow flowers produced in June; 'Frau Dagmar Hastrup' (1) only 1 m (3¼ ft) high, very fragrant, single pale pink flowers opening in June, a good shrub for mass planting; 'F. J. Grootendorst', a thickly-branched shrub only 1 m (3¼ ft) high with shining red flowers borne from June to October; 'Max Graf', a creeping species reaching a maximum height of 50 cm (20 in), with single pink flowers opening in June; and 'White Hedge' (2) about 1.2 m (4 ft) high with snow-white, slightly fragrant flowers which are followed by a profusion of hips.

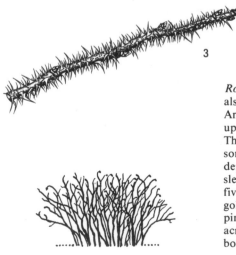

Rosa rugosa is native to the Far East but also grows wild in Europe and North America as a garden escape. It is an upright shrub about 1 m (3¼ ft) high. The branched shoots (3) become later somewhat arching. The young shoots are densely felted, the prickles straight and slender. The compound leaves consist of five to nine wrinkled leaflets, which turn golden-yellow in autumn. The single, pink-red flowers about 7 cm (2¾ in) across are pleasantly scented. They are borne from June to October, so buds and hips (4) can be seen on the same branch. The brick-red, globular hips are somewhat flat with long sepals that formed the calyx. They can be made into tea or jelly.

1

2

4

Common Elder
Sambucus nigra

Caprifoliaceae

A shrub of robust habit, Common Elder is not suitable for a small garden, where it would soon take over the space allotted to other plants. But thanks to its minimal requirements as regards soil and site, elders make excellent shrubs for landscaping. They look well planted in large or small groups. Garden forms with variegated or dissected foliage make good specimen shrubs.

This shrub is best suited in a fertile, fairly moist soil, though it will also succeed in dry soils. It tolerates sun as well as shade, only variegated cultivars needing protection from direct sunlight and severe frosts. It withstands adverse city conditions and its foliage does not attract browsing animals. It is a lime-lover, in contrast with *R. racemosa* (see below), which resents lime in the soil. It is best planted in autumn or spring. Old branches should be cut back to the base. The species is propagated from seeds sown as soon as they are ripe or after stratification in spring. Cultivars with decorative foliage are propagated from softwood cuttings in summer or grafted on to root cuttings.

The Red-berried Elder (*R. racemosa*) occurs widely throughout most of Europe and Asia as far as Northern China. It is a shrub up to 4 m (13 ft) high. Its smooth, grey-brown shoots with numerous longitudinal lenticels have light brown wood. Older branches are grey-brown. The leaves are formed of three to seven ovate-lanceolate leaflets up to 10 cm (4 in) long. The small, yellow-green flowers, which open in April and May, are arranged in dense panicles up to 6 cm (2¹/₄ in) long. They are followed by globular, red berries. The cultivar 'Plumosa Aurea' has finely-dissected golden-yellow leaves.

Common Elder is distributed over almost all Europe and Turkey, growing abundantly in lowlands and foothills up to 1,000 m (3,200 ft) above sea level. It makes a shrub or tree up to 7 m (23 ft) high with grey shoots with large lenticels (2) and grey, deeply-grooved branches with white wood. The leaves are up to 30 cm (1 ft) long and formed of five ovate-lanceolate leaflets that are lighter coloured beneath. The small, five-part yellow-white flowers are arranged in flat umbels (1) up to 20 cm (8 in) across and open in June and July. The fruits are shiny black globular berries (3) containing two flat seeds that mature in September.

Garden forms in cultivation are: 'Aurea',
the Golden-leaved Elder, with
golden-yellow leaves with red stalks;
'Laciniata', Fern-leaved Elder, with
deeply-dissected leaflets; and 'Linearis',
with narrow, almost threadlike leaflets.

Sorbaria
Sorbaria sorbifolia

Rosaceae

Sorbaria sorbifolia is rarely found in cultivation, though it certainly deserves more appreciation from gardeners. It is more often used in parks and large landscaping schemes, where it is planted in groups of different sizes to mask unsightly spots or fill in spaces between taller trees.

Though Sorbarias grow best in well-drained soil and a fairly moist position, they will not fail even in dry soils. They thrive in full sun but tolerate partial shade. Plant bare-rooted plants, preferably in early autumn or spring. To encourage flower formation, cut out the flowered shoots in winter. These shrubs are most easily propagated by division of their abundant suckers. They can also be propagated from root cuttings inserted in a box and stood in a greenhouse, from softwood cuttings and from seeds.

S. aitchisonii is native to Afghanistan, Northern India and Western China. It is an upright shrub up to 3 m (10 ft) high with red shoots and brown branches. The leaves are formed of 13—21 narrowly-lanceolate leaflets up to 8 cm (3¹/₄ in) long, with red petioles. The small, snow-white flowers only about 1 cm (³/₈ in) across are borne in cylindrical panicles up to 25 cm (10 in) long and open in July and August. This species needs winter protection at least during the first winter after planting.

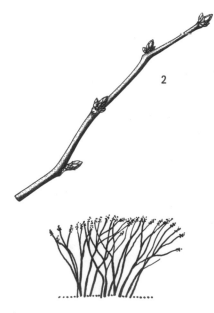

The natural range of *Sorbaria sorbifolia* extends from the Urals to the island of Sakhalin, Kamchatka and Japan. It has spread spontaneously from gardens and parks into the wild over most of Europe and North America. It is an erect deciduous, sparingly-branched shrub about 2 m (6¹/₂ ft) high with the lateral branches sticking out. When planted in a favourable situation, it rapidly spreads by underground suckers to form extensive colonies. The brown young shoots (2) are covered with fine hairs that soon disappear. The leaves are up to 30 cm (1 ft) long and composed of 13—15 lanceolate leaflets tinted bronze when they first develop. The upright or slightly drooping panicles of small, creamy flowers (1) measure about 20 cm (8 in) long and appear in June and July. The fruits are small bladders fused at the base (3).

3

1

191

Bridal Wreath
Spiraea × arguta

Rosaceae

Some 90 species of spiraeas have their homeland in the temperate zone of Europe, Asia and America. *Spiraea × arguta* looks well planted as a single specimen, but is also suitable for growing in large containers. In parks it is planted in groups and widely used to form unclipped hedges. The sprigs with well developed buds can be cut in early spring and put in a vase to bloom.

Spiraea × arguta will withstand extremely dry soil and a polluted environment. It is fully hardy in Britain. It is propagated from hardwood cuttings taken in December, stored in a cool place for the winter, then inserted outdoors the following spring.

S. albiflora is of unknown origin but has been cultivated in Japan for centuries. It is an upright shrub about 50 cm (20 in) high and particularly suitable for a rock garden. Erect umbels of white flowers are borne on the current season's growth in July and August.

S. × cinerea, a hybrid between *S. cana* and *S. hypericifolia*, reaches a height of about 2 m (6¹/₂ ft). Masses of white flowers arranged in umbels appear in May. The particularly hardy cultivar 'Grefsheim' blooms about 10 days earlier than the species.

Spiraea × arguta was produced by hybridising *S. × multiflora* with *S. thunbergii*. It is a dense shrub about 1.8 m (6 ft) high with arching branches. Its dainty young shoots are dark brown, the leaves (1) deciduous and 2—4 cm (³/₄—1¹/₂ in) long. The small,

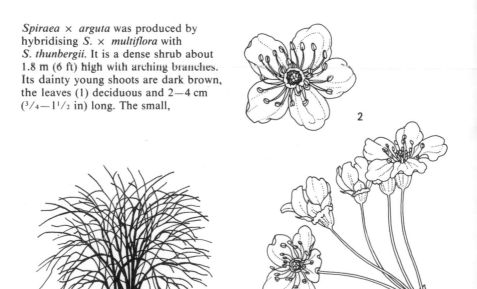

192

snow-white flowers are arranged in
umbels (2) and borne along the shoots
from late April to early May. The fruits
are follicles that split along the inner
suture (3) to reveal 2—10 seeds.

3

1

Spiraea Bumalda hybrids
Spiraea × bumalda   Rosaceae

Spiraea Bumalda hybrids are low-growing shrubs that flower in summer. They are used for mass plantings or underplantings and to make untrimmed hedges. They thrive in humus-rich, well drained, fairly moist soils and bear a profusion of flowers when planted in full sun. They stand up quite well to the polluted atmosphere of industrial regions. They are propagated from hardwood cuttings taken in late autumn.

S. japonica is native to China, Korea and Japan, where it reaches a height of 1.5 m (5 ft), but is much shorter in Britain. Its young shoots are woolly, erect and well branched. Older branches are purple-brown, hairless and striped. The newly sprouted lanceolate leaves are red-brown, later turning a vivid green with grey-green undersides and hairy veins. The small pink flowers with protruding stamens are borne in panicles up to 20 cm (8 in) long. They open in succession from July to September. Widely grown cultivars include: 'Atrosanguinea', with deep pink flowers, 'Ruberrima', up to 1 m (3¹/₄ ft) high, with pink-red flowers; and 'Little Princess', only 50 cm (20 in) high, bearing a profusion of pink-red flowers.

Spiraea × bumalda, a hybrid between *S. albiflora* and *S. japonica*, is an upright, rather densely-branched shrub reaching a maximum of 1 m (3¹/₄ ft) high. Its shoots (2) are angular, the leaves ovate-lanceolate. It flowers from July to August with bluish pink flowers (1) arranged in flat cymes. Its fruits contain tiny elongated seeds (3) and ripen in September. It withstands hard

194

pruning. Many cultivars have proved
their qualities over years of cultivation.
They include: 'Anthony Waterer' (4),
a thickly-branched shrub only 80 cm
(32 in) high, with carmine-pink flowers;
and 'Froebelii', up to 1.2 m (4 ft) high,
with larger flat umbels and more deeply
coloured flowers than the species.

Vanhoutte's Spiraea
Spiraea × vanhouttei   Rosaceae

Vanhoutte's Spiraea makes an elegant specimen shrub for a small garden, while in big gardens and parks it is displayed to good effect when planted in homogenous or mixed groups. It is also grown as a hedging plant. It is a hardy, undemanding shrub, which will tolerate atmospheric pollution. It prefers a sunny or slightly shaded position. It is propagated from hardwood cuttings.

S. menziesii, a North American species, is a shrub up to 1.5 m (5 ft) high, producing many underground runners. Its cylindrical inflorescences formed of carmine-pink flowers open in July and August.

S. nipponica is native to the Japanese island of Honshu. It is an erect shrub up to 2 m (6^1/$_2$ ft) high with arching branches. Its white flowers suffused with red are borne in flat umbels in June and July.

S. prunifolia grows wild in the Chinese province of Hupei, but has spread spontaneously to other parts of China and to Japan. It is an upright shrub up to 2 m (6^1/$_2$ ft) high with thin, broom-like shoots. The double form 'Plena' has white flowers about 1 cm (^{3}/$_8$ in) across, borne on the previous year's wood in May. This shrub is suitable for the warm sunny regions with open well-drained soils that grow good grapes.

S. thunbergii, also a native of China and Japan, is a thickly-branched shrub up to 1.5 m (5 ft) high. It bears a profusion of small, snow-white umbels on the leafless shoots from late April to early May. It also makes a good hedge, as it stands hard clipping.

S. veitchii, native to Central and Western China, is a shrub up to 3.5 m (11^1/$_2$ ft) high with branches arching down to the ground. Its white flowers in broad heads are produced in late June and July.

Vanhoutte's Spiraea (1) is a hybrid between *S. cantoniensis* and *S. trilobata*. It is a twiggy shrub up to 2 m (6^1/$_2$ ft) high with a graceful arching habit. The hairless young shoots (2) are light brown, turning blackish when mature.

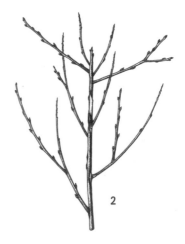

2

The leaves are rather variable in shape so that one branch may carry rhomboidal-ovate as well as three- to five-lobed leaves. They turn orange (3) in autumn before they fall. The previous year's branches are covered with many-flowered corymbs of small, snow-white flowers from late May until the end of June.

3

1

Bladdernut
Staphylea pinnata

Staphyleaceae

The Bladdernut is seldom found in cultivation. It can be planted in groups in parks or as a specimen shrub in small gardens. Pot-grown shrubs used to be forced in January. It prefers a sunny site, though it will also thrive in partial shade. It does well in an open, fertile, limy soil. It can be damaged by frost during a severe winter but will rapidly grow again in spring. As it has a well-developed root system, the Bladdernut is best planted bare-rooted. Water liberally during summer droughts. No regular pruning is necessary. The species are propagated from stratified seeds in spring. Low-growing species are mostly propagated from softwood cuttings inserted in a propagator in summer. Propagation from one-year-old layers is also possible.

S. colchica grows wild in the western Caucasus, making a sparsely-branched shrub up to 4 m (13 ft) high. The three- to five-lobed leaves are formed of leaflets up to 8 cm (3¹/₄ in) long. The fragrant, yellow-white flowers are borne in erect panicles up to 10 cm (4 in) high. This species flowers in late May and is particularly suitable for sunny places on open soils that suit vines.

S. bumalda grows wild in China and Korea as well as Japan. It is only 2 m (6¹/₂ ft) high, with trifoliate leaves formed of 3—6 cm (1¹/₄—2¹/₄ in) long leaflets. The sparse, erect clusters of yellow-white flowers are up to 7 cm (2³/₄ in) long and appear in June.

S. × elegans, obtained by hybridising *S. colchica* and *S. pinnata*, is a shrub some 4 m (13 ft) high, with long, drooping inflorescences of flowers with white petals and pink calyces. They appear from late April till the end of May. The fruits are seldom produced in our climate.

Staphylea pinnata (1) is native to Central and Southern Europe and Turkey, extending to the warmer parts of the Caucasus. It is a shrub with oblong-ovate head, reaching a height of about 4 m (13 ft). Its young shoots (2) are olive-green, older branches dark brown with elongated lenticels. The leaves are formed of five to seven ovate leaflets measuring up to 9 cm (3¹/₂ in) long. The yellow-white flowers are borne in drooping axillary clusters up to 12 cm (4³/₄ in) long. This shrub blooms from late May to the end of June. The fruits are globular, membranous capsules (3) containing several seeds that are used to make folk jewellery.

1

2

3

199

Snowberry
Symphoricarpos albus
(syn. *S. racemosus*)

Caprifoliaceae

The Snowberry is widely used to make informal as well as clipped hedges. It is often planted under taller trees, as it can bear deep shade and rapidly spreads by underground suckers. Depending on the site, this makes it a troublesome weed or an excellent pioneering plant for covering dumps and other wasteland. In landscaping it is a suitable plant for masking sheer slopes. Snowberries are much visited by bees when in flower. Their thick branches provide shelter for nesting birds. Remember that their fruits contain poisonous substances that can cause sickness, particularly in children.

Snowberries thrive in full sun as well as shade. The more sunlight they are given, the more profusely they flower. They will succeed in dry as well as damp soils. They are hardy in our climate and tolerate a smoke-filled city environment. They are best planted in autumn or early spring while the plants are dormant. Remove any old branches that are causing overcrowding. Hedges are clipped in late winter and, if necessary, in summer.

Symphoricarpos albus is propagated from hardwood cuttings. The cuttings are taken in autumn and inserted in the open ground in a sheltered position. The low-growing species are also propagated from softwood cuttings. The species itself is increased from stratified seeds sown in spring.

Symphoricarpos albus (1) is a North American species, growing on dry, stony hillsides from the Atlantic to the Pacific. It has become naturalized in Europe as a garden escape.

It makes a twiggy shrub up to 1.8 m (6 ft) high with dainty, slightly arching branches. The young shoots (2) are thin and yellow-brown, older stems are grey-brown. The fruit-bearing branches carry orbicular-ovate leaves up to 5 cm

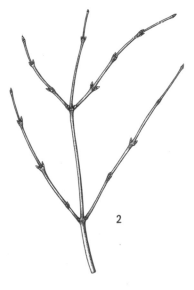

2

(2 in) long, while the suckers are covered with three-lobed leaves finely felted beneath. The small, bell-shaped, white-pink flowers (3) arranged in racemes or spikes open in succession from June to September. The fruits are globular berries (4) each containing two seeds. The variety *S. rivularis* bears short racemes of flowers and a profusion of berries.

CAUTION: The fruits are poisonous and can cause digestive problems in children.

Chenault's Snowberry
Symphoricarpos × chenaultii   Caprifoliaceae

Chenault's Snowberry is a rather low-growing shrub, generally used to clothe large areas of land with green foliage. Its salient feature is its pink-red berries. It is rather more demanding than *S. albus* (see previous page), doing best in an open, fertile, reasonably moist soil. This species also spreads extensively to swamp other, more delicate woody plants.

    S. × doorenbosii, (syn. S. hybrids), is a hybrid between *S. × albus* var. *rivularis* and *S. chenaultii.* This group comprises many attractive cultivars similar in habit to *S. albus* but with berries in various shades of red. They include: 'Erect', of upright habit, with dense racemes of pink flowers and mahogany-red berries maturing as early as July, and 'Mother of Pearl', about 1.5 m (5 ft) high, with pearl-pink berries ripening in late September.

    S. orbiculatus (syn. *S. vulgaris*) is a North American shrub only 1.5 m (5 ft) high. Its erect branches arch over as they mature. The grey-brown shoots are covered with short, velvety hairs. The widely ovate, woolly leaves are 4—7 cm ($1^{1}/_{2}$—$2^{1}/_{4}$ in) long, grey-green on the underside, and turn orange-red in the autumn. It blooms from July to September with pinkish green flowers in dense racemes. The fruits are small and purple-red. The cultivar 'Variegatus' has golden-yellow margins to the leaves and grows slower than the species.

Chenault's Snowberry (1) was produced by crossing *S. microphyllus* with *S. orbiculatus.* It makes a shrub about 1.2 m (4 ft) high. The shoots are much longer, but are rather weak, so the shrub develops a somewhat creeping habit. The reddish shoots are clothed with fine hairs. The ovate to elliptic leaves about 2 cm ($^{3}/_{4}$ in) long are hairy on both sides. The small, pink bell flowers are arranged in terminal and lateral spikes and appear in June and July. They are followed by pinkish red berries (2), often spotted with white. The cultivar 'Hancock' is a thickly-branched shrub of almost creeping habit, only 50 cm (20 in) high. It is an ideal plant for covering large areas of bare ground, as it tolerates shady places and its arching branches readily root whenever they touch the ground (3).

CAUTION: The fruits may contain poisonous substances.

1

Rouen Lilac
Syringa × *chinensis*

Oleaceae

Syringa × *chinensis* ranks high among ornamental shrubs and is often planted in parks, gardens and housing estates. It makes a lovely specimen shrub but is also striking when planted in groups.

Just like other type species it will grow in almost any slightly limy garden soil, provided it is not too dry or waterlogged. It stands up well to a polluted atmosphere and its foliage does not attract browsing animals. Best time for planting is autumn. Set the plant deeper in the soil than it grew in the nursery. Remove flowered shoots promptly to prevent seed formation. Thin out older shrubs now and then to encourage new vigorous shoots to develop.

Nurseries propagate *S.* × *chinensis* by grafting on to seedlings of *S. vulgaris*, as the hybrid rarely produces suckers and bears no fruits. Softwood cuttings should be inserted in a cold frame in June. Hardwood cuttings also root quite readily.

S. josikaea (the Hungarian Lilac) is native to South-eastern Europe. It is an erect shrub reaching a height of 4 m (13 ft) and producing only a few underground suckers. Its dark violet flowers borne in erect, narrow, faintly fragrant panicles up to 20 cm (8 in) long, open in May and June.

S. reflexa, a species from Central China, is a rather wide-spreading shrub up to 4 m (13 ft) high. Its carmine buds develop into dark pink flowers in drooping panicles up to 15 cm (6 in) long and open in late June.

Syringa × *chinensis* is a random hybrid between *S.* × *persica* and *S. vulgaris*, produced in 1774 in Rouen, France. It is a rather sparsely-branched shrub of arching habit, growing to a height of about 4 m (13 ft). Its young shoots are grey-brown with prominent lenticels (2). Older branches are grey. The leaves are narrowly ovate to lanceolate, and about 6 cm (2¹/₄ in) long. Masses of faintly fragrant, lilac-pink flowers are arranged in sparse, somewhat drooping panicles up to 25 cm (10 in) long. A few cultivars are offered by specialist nurseries, the most widely grown being 'Metensis', with lilac-pink flowers, and 'Saugeana' (1), with lilac-red flowers.

1

2

205

Syringa Vulgaris hybrids

Oleaceae

Hundreds of cultivars are listed as Syringa Vulgaris hybrids. They differ in habit of growth, the type of inflorescence, colour and size of flowers and the intensity of their fragrance. In gardens they are planted as specimen shrubs or in groups, occasionally as trees. White cultivars are forced in greenhouses to produce flowers during the winter.

The following cultivars are most often offered by specialized nurseries and garden centres: 'Souvenir de Louis Späth' (1), with single, purple-red flowers in panicles up to 30 cm (1 ft) long; 'Charles Joly', with double, purplish red flowers with lighter undersides to the petals; 'Charles X' (2), with single, violet flowers; 'Katharine Havemeyer', with large, double cobalt flowers suffused with lilac; 'Maréchal Foch', early-flowering, with single, lilac-pink flowers and carmine buds; 'Marie Legraye', with single pure white flowers in dense panicles; 'Michel Buchner', with double lilac flowers with white centres; 'Mme Antoine Buchner', with double mallow-pink flowers; 'Mme Lemoine', with large double pure white flowers; 'Mrs. Edward Harding', with double pale purplish red flowers, and 'Primrose', with single pale primrose-yellow flowers.

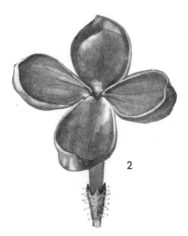

2

206

Syringa vulgaris grows wild in stony, open, but reasonably moist soils in the warm parts of the Balkans, from where it has spread naturally to Central Europe and Asia. It is a well branched shrub or tree up to 5 m (17 ft) high, spreading extensively by underground suckers. Its one-year-old shoots (3) are olive-green, older branches are grey with the bark peeling off in vertical strips. The heart-shaped leaves are up to 10 cm (4 in) long. It flowers in May with single, pink-blue, very fragrant flowers arranged in panicles up to 20 cm (8 in) long. The fruits are flattened two-valved leathery capsules (4) about 1 cm ($^3/_8$ in) long, splitting open to reveal two flat seeds, each rimmed with membranous wings. Shoots that have flowered and faded look unpleasant and untidy, so should be promptly removed.

207

Tamarisk
Tamarix tetrandra
Tamaricaceae

Tamarisks make exotic-looking growth. As they are difficult to fit in with other woody plants, they are best planted as specimen shrubs in grass. In some places, especially by the sea where the climate is favourable, they are used to make hedges. They are quite undemanding shrubs, happy in sunny places and fairly light, deep, well-drained soils containing only a little lime. They tolerate salty soils, droughts and strong winds quite well. Cut back any shoots damaged by frost during a severe winter so the shrub makes new growth from the base. Plant only young, container-grown plants, as older specimens are reluctant to establish. Before planting, cut back the top growth hard and soak the root ball in a pail of water for several hours. Tamarisks are propagated from hardwood cuttings inserted in a frame in March or from softwood cuttings in a propagator in summer.

T. parviflora is native to South-eastern Europe. It is a shrub up to 4 m (13 ft) high, with slender, pendulous, red-brown shoots and dark brown older branches. The pale pink flowers in racemes up to 4 cm (1 1/2 in) long appear on the previous year's branches as early as May.

T. pentandra is native to South-eastern Europe and the Orient and makes a shrub or tree up to 4 m (13 ft) high. Its young shoots are green, the older red-brown branches bear pink-red flowers in thickly-branched panicles up to 50 cm (20 in) long. It blooms in July and August. The cultivar 'Rubra' has pink-red flowers.

The natural range of *Tamarix tetrandra* (1) extends from Greece and Cyprus to Turkey and the Crimea. It is a small tree or shrub some 3 m (10 ft) high. Its black-brown shoots (2) are twiggy and pendulous, older branches dark brown and erect. The small lateral branchlets with scale-like leaflets are shed in autumn. Leaflets borne on the older persistent branches are needle-shaped and arranged in spirals and like heather leaflets. The pale pink flowers (3)

appear on the previous season's growth before the leaves, in late April and May. They are arranged in lateral racemes and give off a pleasant, spicy scent. The fruits are small 3—4 valved capsules containing many finely hairy seeds.

209

Winter-flowering Viburnum
Viburnum farreri
(syn. *V. fragrans*)

Caprifoliaceae

The genus *Viburnum* comprises over 100 species classed in nine groups, mostly originating in the temperate and sub-tropical zones of the Northern Hemisphere. This viburnum belongs to the subgroup 'Thyrsoma'. It is a most valuable shrub, as it blooms in late winter and even in autumn when other flowers are rare in the garden. This shrub with its sweetly-scented flowers makes a superb specimen planted on a lawn or among perennials. It can also be planted in groups in parks, modern housing estates and similar places.

This shrub appreciates a slightly sheltered, warm position and a deep, well-drained but reasonably moist soil. It thrives in full sun and tolerates semi-shade, but should be protected from winter sunshine. It will grow in the polluted atmosphere of industrial districts.

Though this viburnum can be planted bare-rooted in autumn or early spring, try to buy container-grown plants, as they can be planted at any time of year provided the soil is not frost-bound or excessively wet. They grow very slowly. Pruning, if any, should be carried out soon after flowering, as this species flowers on the previous year's wood. Viburnums are readily propagated from cuttings. They can also be propagated from suckers or one-year-old layers.

Viburnum farreri (1) is native to the Chinese provinces of Hupei and Kansu. It is a well-branched, slow-growing shrub of upright habit, reaching a maximum of 3 m (10 ft) high. Its red-brown shoots (3) carry elliptic leaves

3

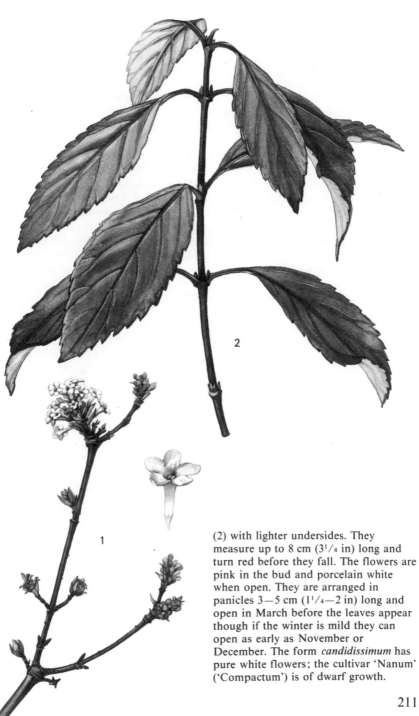

1

2

(2) with lighter undersides. They measure up to 8 cm (3¼ in) long and turn red before they fall. The flowers are pink in the bud and porcelain white when open. They are arranged in panicles 3—5 cm (1¼—2 in) long and open in March before the leaves appear though if the winter is mild they can open as early as November or December. The form *candidissimum* has pure white flowers; the cultivar 'Nanum' ('Compactum') is of dwarf growth.

Wayfaring Tree
Viburnum lantana

Caprifoliaceae

Viburnum lantana belongs to the subgroup 'Lantana'. All viburnums of this subgroup are planted as single specimens or in groups on a lawn or under taller trees. They are also suitable for cultivation in pots or on a rock garden. They are slow-growing and are better not pruned. Propagate them from suckers or cuttings. Hybrids are budded on to *V. lantana* rootstocks in summer.

This subgroup comprises the following species:

V. carlesii, a native of Japan and Korea, is a slow-growing shrub reaching a maximum height of 1.2 m (4 ft). The young shoots are hairy, old branches are hairless. Its widely ovate leaves up to 10 cm (4 in) long are lighter beneath and felted on both sides. They turn yellow-red in autumn. Hemispherical umbels of flowers up to 7 cm ($2^3/_4$ in) across open in April and May. The pink buds develop into very fragrant, porcelain white flowers.

V. × burkwoodii, a hybrid between *V. carlesii* and *V. utile*, is a sparse shrub up to 2 m ($6^1/_2$ ft) high, with glossy leaves and sweetly-scented umbels of pinkish white flowers. It blooms in April and May with sometimes a repeat flowering in autumn. The cultivar 'Park Farm Hybrid' flowers later with inflorescences up to 12 cm ($4^3/_4$ in) across.

V. × carlcephalum was produced by crossing *V. carlesii* with *V. macrocephalum*. It reaches a height of about 1.5 m (5 ft). The leaves are up to 12 cm ($4^3/_4$ in) long. Umbels of pure white flowers open in April and May and are richly scented.

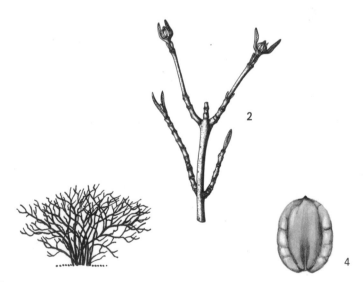

212

The Wayfaring Tree (1) is native to
Southern Europe and Turkey, where it
grows on sunny, limy slopes. It is
a wide-spreading shrub about 3 m (10 ft)
high with arching branches. Its young
shoots (2) are felted grey, older branches
turn yellowish brown. It flowers in May
and June. The velvety white flowers
are arranged in umbels about 10 cm
(4 in) across. The fruit is a flattened
red drupe (3) about 8 mm ($^5/_{16}$ in) in
diameter, turning shiny black as it ripens
(stone — 4).

213

Guelder Rose
Viburnum opulus
Caprifoliaceae

Guelder Roses are popular shrubs, generally planted as single specimens or in groups in gardens, parks, on housing estates and in public grounds. In landscaping they are used to cover bare slopes along motorways and to anchor soil on river banks. Thickets of Guelder Roses are attractive to nesting birds. They need a moist position, as on dry sites they are infested by leaf aphids and caterpillars. Guelder Roses tolerate partial shade, but flower more profusely in full sun. Barerooted plants are planted in autumn or early spring. Cut back poorly branched specimens to encourage new shoots to develop in spring.

Viburnum opulus is propagated from seeds which are sown after harvesting or stratified and sown the following spring. Cultivars can be propagated from hardwood cuttings in winter, softwood cuttings in spring, or one-year-old layers.

V. sargentii, also a member of the subgroup 'Opulus', grows wild on mountain slopes and in thin woodland in Japan and Northern and North-eastern China. It is a shrub of compact habit, reaching about 3 m (10 ft) high. Its umbels of creamy white flowers are about 10 cm (4 in) across and open in May to July. The marginal, sterile flowers are some 3 cm (1¼ in) wide. A profusion of orange-red berries containing whitish seeds follows.

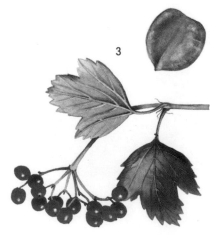

3

Viburnum opulus is distributed throughout most of Europe, North Africa, Turkey, Caucasus and Siberia, where it usually grows in damp places along rivers in the lowlands and foothills. It is an upright, irregularly-branched shrub about 3 m (10 ft) high. The yellow-brown young shoots (2) turn ash-grey as they mature. The three- to five-lobed leaves up to 12 cm ($4^3/_4$ in) long turn yellow, orange or red in autumn before they fall. Flat umbels up to 10 cm (4 in) across appear in May and June and are formed of small white flowers surrounded by large sterile white flowers that are pleasantly scented. The ovate, coral-red fruits, each containing one stone (3), ripen in late September. The cultivars 'Sterile' ('Roseum') (1) bears only sterile flowers. These are greenish white, ageing to a pinkish colour.

Weigela
Weigela florida
(syn. W. rosea)

Caprifoliaceae

The genus *Weigela* comprises 12 species, mostly from Eastern Asia. The North American species originally included in this genus are nowadays classed in the separate genus *Diervilla*.

Weigelas are planted in homogeneous or mixed groups in parks or large gardens and also make good specimen shrubs for small gardens. They are grown as informal hedging plants too. Modest in their requirements, weigelas are tolerant of smoky city conditions. They are happy in a well-drained, humus-rich fertile soil on the moist side, preferably acid or mildly alkaline. A light, sunny site is essential for abundant flowering, though weigelas tolerate partial shade. Plant them bare-rooted in autumn or spring. Cut back the oldest branches to just above ground level every two or three years to encourage new shoots to develop, as these produce the best flowers. Shrubs that are too old can be rejuvenated by heavy pruning. The stems can be damaged by severe black frosts, but the shrub will rapidly make new growth from the roots. Even quite old bushes stand replanting provided it is done while they are dormant.

Weigelas are most readily propagated from cuttings. The lush-growing species and cultivars can be propagated from hardwood cuttings, others from softwood cuttings from mid-May to mid-June inserted under plastic in a propagator. The species can be increased from seed sown in trays in spring and later pricked out into sheltered beds. The seedlings are rather variable in their characteristics, however.

Weigela florida (1) has its homeland in Northern China, Japan and Korea. It is a shrub some 2.5 m (8¹/₂ ft) high, with red-brown, woolly shoots (2) and grey-brown branches with peeling bark. The leaves are elliptical, up to 8 cm (3¹/₄ in) long, with lighter undersides. The funnel-shaped, carmine-pink flowers with light centres are borne in three- or four-flowered clusters from the second

1

half of May till the end of June. Some
specimens flower a second time later in
the season. The fruits are two-valved
woody capsules splitting to reveal
angular seeds that are frequently
wingless (3).

The cultivar 'Foliis Purpureis' (4),
only 1.2 m (4 ft) high and of compact
habit, bears brown-red leaves and deep
pink flowers. 'Variegata' reaches
a height of about 1.5 m (5 ft). Its leaves
are irregularly bordered with creamy
white, its flowers are a deep pink.

217

Weigela hybrids

The name Weigela hybrids covers the crosses made between Weigela species native to the countries of the Far East. Though hybridizing has yielded almost 200 cultivars, only a handful of these are offered by specialized nurseries and garden centres. Most commonly grown are: 'Bristol Ruby', a lush-growing, late-flowering shrub up to 3 m (10 ft) high, with red-suffused carmine flowers that flowers again in the autumn; 'Eva Rathke' (2), a low-growing variety only 1.5 m (5 ft) high, slow-growing, flowering continuously from May onwards with deep crimson flowers; 'Newport Red' (1), a lush-growing cultivar 2—3 m (6$^1/_2$—10 ft) high, with large, deep red flowers and 'Styriaca' (3), an early- and profuse-flowering shrub 2—3 m (6$^1/_2$—10 ft) high. Its flowers are pinkish red.

W. japonica, native to China and Japan, is a shrub some 3 m (10 ft) high, that flowers in May and June. The stalked flowers with short stigmas are light pink as they open, later turning a deeper colour.

W. praecox, a native of Korea and North-eastern China, is an erect, thickly-branched shrub some 2 m (6$^1/_2$ ft) high. Its yellow-suffused, purplish pink flowers appear as early as the beginning of May.

Weigela hybrids form shrubs with semi-arching branches. They vary in height from 1.5 to 3 m (5—10 ft), depending on the particular cultivar. The young shoots (4) are slender and greenish in colour, later turning grey-brown and fleshy. The lanceolate, serrate leaves with short petioles measure 5—12 cm (2—4$^3/_4$ in) long. The funnel-shaped flowers up to 3 cm (1$^1/_4$ in) long are borne singly or in few-flowered inflorescences on the lateral shoots growing from the previous year's wood. They appear from the second half of May till the end of June. Some cultivars bear single flowers even later. The hybrid weigelas generally produce larger and more conspicuous flowers than the species. The flowers can vary in colour from white, yellow and pink to red and purple.

219

INDEX

Numbers in bold type refer to main entries

Acacia, False 180
— Rose 20, 21, **180, 181**
Acer 7, 8, 21
— *campestre* 23
— *japonicum* 28
— *palmatum* 13, 20, 26, **28, 29**
Aesculus 20, 21
— *parviflora* **30, 31**
— *pavia* 30
Allspice, Carolina 20, 21, **46, 47**
Almond, Dwarf Russian 162
Amorpha canescens 32
— *fruticosa* **32, 33**
— *microphylla* 32
— *nana* 32
Amorpha 21
Angelica Tree **34, 35**
— Chinese 20, 34
Aralia 10, 13, 17, 20
— *chinensis* 34
— *elata* 34
— *spinosa* **34, 35**
Ash, Flowering 60
Azalea pontica **170, 171**
Azalea 20, 25, 26, **170, 171**
— Ghent 171

Barberry 9, 13
— Common 36
— Thunberg's 20, 21, 23, 25, **36, 37**
Beauty Bush 14, 20, 22, 25, **128, 129**
Berberis 9, 13, 20, 21, 23, 25
— *aggregata* 36
— *buxifolia* 26
— × *ottawensis* 36
— × *rubrostilla* 36
— *thunbergii* × *Berberis vulgaris* 36
Berberis, Holly-leaved **144, 145**
Betula humilis 38
— *nana* 26, **38, 39**
— *pumila* 38
Birch 10
— Dwarf **38, 39**
Blackthorn **160, 161**
Bladdernut 20, 22, **198, 199**
Box, Common 23, 24, 26, **44, 45**
Box Thorn 22, **140, 141**
— Chinese 10, 140
Briar, Austrian **184, 185**
Bridal Wreath **192, 193**
Broom 9, 10, 12, 20, **104, 105**
— Common **86, 87**
— Warminster 25, **84, 85**
Buckeye, Bottlebrush 20, 21, **30, 31**

— Red 30
Buckthorn, Alder 168
— Common 21, 22, **168, 169**
— Sea 10, 20, 22, 25, **116, 117**
Buddleia 21
— *alternifolia* 20, **40, 41**
— *davidii* 40, **42, 43**
Buddleia 10, 13, 15, 17, **40, 41**
Butterfly Bush 21, **42, 43**
Buxus 23, 24, 26
— *microphylla* 44
— *sempervirens* **44, 45**

Calycanthus 20, 21
— *fertilis* 46
— *floridus* **46, 47**
— *glaucus* 46
Caragana 21, 23
— *arborescens* **48, 49**
— *frutescens* 48
— *frutex* 48
— *pygmea* 48
Carpinus 7, 23
Caryopteris 17
— × *clandonensis* **50, 51**
— *incana* 50
— *mastacanthus* 50
— *mongolica* 50
— *tangutica* 50
Ceanothus 9, 12
— *americanus* 52
— *coeruleus* 52
— hybrids **52, 53**
— *ovatus* 52
Cercis 9, 20
— *canadensis* **54, 55**
— *chinensis* 54
— *siliquastrum* 54
Chaenomeles 13, 14, 21, 23—26
— *alpina* 57
— hybrids **58, 59**
— *japonica* **56, 57**, 58
— *lagenaria* 56
— *speciosa* 56, 58
— × *superba* **58, 59**
Cherry 13, 19, 20
— Cornelian **66, 67**
— Japanese Flowering 21
Cherry Laurel **158, 159**
Chionanthus 20, 21
— *retusus* 60, 61
— *virginicus* **60, 61**
Cinquefoil 7
— Shrubby 20, 22—26, **156, 157**

220

Cobnut, Purple 70
Colutea 13, 21
— *arborescens* **62, 63**
— *cruenta* 62
— × *media* 62
— *orientalis* 62
Cornus 10, 20, 21, 23
— *alba* **64, 65**
— *alternifolia* 68
— *amomum* 64
— *brachypoda* 66
— *florida* 66
— *kousa* 66
— *macrophylla* 66
— *mas* 19, **66, 67**
— *nuttallii* 68
— *sanguinea* **68, 69**
— *stolonifera* 68
Corylus 7, 10, 21, 26
— *avellana* **70, 71**
— *maxima* 70
Cotinus 9, 20, 21, 25
— *coggyria* **72, 73**
Cotoneaster 7, 13
— *adpressus* 26, **74, 75**
— *bullatus* 76
— *calocarpus* 81
— *congestus* 76
— *conspicuus* 76
— *dammeri* 24—26, **76, 77**
— *dielsianus* 76
— *divaricatus* 78
— *franchetii* 78
— *frigidus* 80
— *henryanus* 80
— *horizontalis* 75, **78, 79**
— *microphyllus* 78
— *moupinensis* 78
— *multiflorus* 20, 21, **80, 81**
— *praecox* 80
— *radicans* 76
— *rugosus* 80
— *salicifolius* 80
— × *watereri* 80
Cotoneaster 7, 14, 16, 20, 25, **74, 75**
— Fishbone 26, **78, 79**
— Watereri Hybrids 80
Crab apple 13, 20, **146, 147**
— Hybrids 22, 25
— Siberian 146
Crataegus 10, 13, 14, 20, 21, 23
— *crus-galli* 82
— *monogyna* 82
— *oxyacantha* **82, 83**
Currant, Alpine 22, 23,25
— Flowering 13, 16
— Golden 178
— Mountain **176, 177**

— Red Flowering **178, 179**
Cydonia maulei **56, 57**
Cydonia **56, 57**
Cytisus 9, 10, 12, 20
— *ardoini* 86
— *decumbens* 26, 84
— × *kewensis* 86
— *multiflorus* 84, 86
— *nigricans* 84, 86
— × *praecox* 25, **84, 85**
— *purgans* 84
— *purpureus* 86
— *scoparius* 84, **86, 87**

Daphne 9, 10, 14, 20, 21, 26
— × *burkwoodii* 88
— *caucasica* × *Daphne cneorum* 88
  cneorum 88
— *mezereum* **88, 89**
Deutzia crenata **92, 93**
— *discolor* 92
— *gracilis* 90
— × *hybrida* 90
— *longifolia* 92
— × *magnifica* 92
— *purpurascens* 90
— × *rosea* 20, 21, **90, 91**
— *scabra* **92, 93**
— *vilmiriniae* 92
Deutzia 9, 10, **90—93**
Dogwood 10
— Flowering 66
— Red **68, 69**
— White 21, 23, **64, 65**
— Dyer's Greenweed 20, 24—26, **104, 105**

Elaeagnus 9, 10, 20, 21
— *angustifolia* 94
— *commutata* **94, 95**
— *pungens* 94
— *umbellata* 94
Elder, Common 10, 22, **188, 189**
— Fern-leaved 189
— Golden-leaved 189
— Red-berried 188
Elm 7
Erica 16
Euonymus 7, 10, 20, 21
— *alatus* 96
— *europaeus* **96, 97**
— *phellomanus* 96
Exochorda 13, 20, 21
— *albertii* 98
— *giraldii* 98
— *grandiflora* **98, 99**
— *korolkowii* 98
— × *macrantha* 98
— *racemosa* **98, 99**

221

Exochorda wilsonii 98

Filbert 70
Firethorn 20, 22—25, **166, 167**
Forsythia fortunei 102
— × *intermedia* 20, 22, 23, 25, **100, 101**
— *ovata* 102
— *sieboldii* 102
— *suspensa* 16, 100, **102, 103**
— *viridissima* 100, 102
Forsythia 9, 10, 13
Fraxinus ornus 60
Fringe Tree 20, **60, 61**
— Chinese 60
— White 21
Fuchsia 17

Garland Flower 88
Genista 20, 24—26
— *hispanica* 104
— *pilosa* 104
— *radiata* 104
— *tinctoria* **104, 105**
Golden Bell Tree **100, 101**
Golden Rain **130, 131**
Gorse, Spanish 104
Greenweed, Dyer's 20, 24—26, **104, 105**
Guelder Rose **214, 215**

Halesia 9, 20
— *carolina* **106, 107**
— *diptera* 106, 107
— *monticola* 106
— *tetraptera* **106, 107**
Hamamelis 9, 10, 12—14, 20, 22
— × *intermedia* 110
— *japonica* **108, 109**, 110
— *japonica* var. *arborea* 109
— *japonica* var. *flavopurpurascens* 109
— *macrophylla* 112
— *mollis* **110, 111**
— *vernalis* 112
— *virginiana* 108, **112, 113**
Hawthorn 10, 13, 14, **82, 83**
— Cockspur 82
— Common White 82
— English 20, 21, 23
Hazel 7, 10
— Common 21, **70, 71**
— Corkscrew 26, 71
— Witch *see* Witch Hazel
Heather 16
Hercules' Club **34, 35**
Hibiscus 10, 13, 19, 20, 22, 23, 25
— *syriacus* **114, 115**
Hippophae 10, 20, 22, 25
— *rhamnoides* **116, 117**
— *salicifolia* 116
Holly 7, 22

— Common 20, **124, 125**
— English 22, 23
Honeysuckle, Tartar 8, 22, **138, 139**
Hop Tree 22, **164, 165**
Hornbeam 7, 22, 23
Hydrangea arborescens **118, 119**
— *macrophylla* 120
— *paniculata* **120, 121**
— *sargentiana* 120
Hydrangea 9, 10, 13
— Sargent's 120
— Snowhill 20, 22, 25
Hypericum 10, 13, 24—26
— *androsaemum* 122
— *calycinum* 122
hookeranum 122
— × *moseranum* 122
— *patulum* **122, 123**

Ilex 7, 20, 22, 23
— *aquifolium* **124, 125**
— *verticillata* 124
Indigo False **32, 33**

Judas Tree 9, 20, 54

Kerria japonica **126, 127**, 172
Kerria 10, 22
Kolkwitzia 10, 14, 20, 22, 25
— *amabilis* **128, 129**

Laburnum 10, 13, 21
— *alpinum* 130
— *anagyroides* **130, 131**
— *vulgare* **130, 131**
— × *watereri* 130
Laburnum, Common 20, 22, 25, **130, 131**
— Scotch 130
Ligustrum 10, 22—24
— *amurense* 134
— *obtusifolium* 134
— *ovalifolium* **132, 133**, 135
— *sinense* 134
— *vulgare* **134, 135**
Lilac 10, 13, 16, 19, 20, 22
— Californian 9, **52, 53**
— Hungarian 204
— Rouen **204, 205**
Lime, Small-leaved 23
Liriodendron tulipifera **136, 137**
Lonicera 8, 22
— *korolkowii* 138
— *maackii* 138
— *tatarica* **138, 139**
Lycium 10, 22
— *barbarum* **140, 141**
— *chinense* 140
— *halimifolium* **140, 141**

Magnolia denudata 142

222

Magnolia gracilis **142, 143**
— *kobus* 20, **142, 143**
— *liliiflora* 142
— × *soulangiana* 142
— *stellata* 142
— *tomentosa* **142, 143**
Magnolia 8—10, 12, **142, 143**
Mahonia aquifolium **144, 145**
— *japonica* 144
Mahonia 22, 24, 25, **144, 145**
Mallow, Jew's **126, 127**
— Rose 13, 19, 20, 22, 23, 25, **114, 115**
Malus 13, 20, 22, 25, **146, 147**
— × *adstringens* 147
— *baccata* 146
— *coronaria* 147
— *floribunda* 146
— *prunifolia* 146
— × *purpurea* 147
Maple 7, 8, 10, 21
— Field 23
— Japanese **28, 29**
Mezereon 9, 10, 13, 20, 21, 26, **88, 89**
Mock Orange 8, 10, 13, 19, 22, 23, **150, 151**
Moutan **148, 149**

Ninebark 22, 23, **154, 155**

Oleaster 9, 10, 20, 21, **94, 95**
Olive, Wild **94, 95**
Oregon Grape **144, 145**
Paeonia 8
— *delavayi* 148
— *lactiflora* 148
— *lutea* 148
— *suffruticosa* 26, **148, 149**
Papaver 21
Pea Shrub, Siberian 21
Pea Tree 23, **48, 49**
Peach 162
Pearl Bush 13, 20, 21, **98, 99**
Periwinkle 24
Philadelphus 8, 10, 13, 19, 22, 23
— *coronarius* **150, 151**, 152
— *microphyllus* 152
— *nivalis* 152
— × *purpureo-maculatus* 152
— × *virginalis* **152, 153**
Philadelphus Lemoine hybrids 153
— Purpureo-maculatus hybrids 152
— Virginalis hybrids **152, 153**
Physocarpus 22, 23
— *amurensis* 154
— *opulifolius* **154, 155**
Poppy 21
Potentilla 7, 20, 22—26
— *fruticosa* **156, 157**

Privet 10, 22, **132, 133**
— Common 23, 24, **134, 135**
Prunus 13, 21, 22
— *cerasifera* 160
— *laurocerasus* **158, 159**
— *persica* 162
— *spinosa* **160, 161**
— *tenella* 162
— *triloba* 14, 26, **162, 163**
— *triloba* var. *simplex* 163
Ptelea trifoliata **164, 165**
Pyracantha 20, 22—25
— *coccinea* **166, 167**

Quince, Dwarf 56
— Flowering 13, 14, **56, 57**
— Japanese 26, 56
— Ornamental **58, 59**
Quince hybrids 21, 23—25

Redbud **54, 55**
Rhamnus 21, 22
— *cathartica* **168, 169**
— *frangula* 168
Rhododendron luteum **170, 171**
Rhododendron 9, 16, **170, 171**
Rhodotypos scandens **172, 173**
Rhodotypos 22, **172, 173**
Rhus cotinus **72, 73**
— *typhina* 12, 16, 17, 20, 25, **174, 175**
Ribes 13, 16, 22, 23, 25
— *alpinum* **176, 177**
— *americanum* 178
— *aureum* 176, 178
— *multiflorum* 178
— *sanguineum* 176, **178, 179**
Robinia 7, 20, 21
— *hispida* **180, 181**
— *pseudoacacia* 180
Rosa 20, 22
— *canina* **182, 183**
— *foetida* **184, 185**
— *hugonis* 184
— *lutea* **184, 185**
— *omeiensis* 184
— *pimpinellifolia* 184
— *rugosa* 26, **186, 187**
— *spinosissima* 184
— *xanthina* 184
Rose 10, 14
— Burnet 184
— Dog 20, 22, **182, 183**
— Guelder 22, 26, **214, 215**
— Japanese Apple 26
— Mount Omei 184
— Pere Hugo's 184
— Ramanas **186, 187**
— Scotch 184
Rose of Sharon **122, 123**

223

Rowan 21

Salix 7
Sambucus 10, 22
 — *nigra* **188, 189**
 — *racemosa* 188
Sarothamnus scoparius **86, 87**
Senna, Bladder 13, 21, **62, 63**
Silver Bell, Carolina **106, 107**
Sloe 20, 22, **160, 161**
Smoke Bush 9, 21, 25, **72, 73**
Smoke Plant 20
Snowberry 16, 21—23, **200, 201**
 — Chenault's 24, **202, 203**
Snowdrop Tree 20, **106, 107**
Sorbaria aitchisonii 190
 — *sorbifolia* **190, 191**
Sorbaria 22, **190, 191**
Sorbus 21
Spindle Tree 7, 10
 — European 20, 21, **96, 97**
Spiraea albiflora 192, 194
 — × *arbuta* **192, 193**
 — × *bumalda* 13, 24, **194, 195**
 — *cana* 192
 — *cantoniensis* 196
 — × *cinerea* 192
 — *hypericifolia* 192
 — *japonica* 194
 — *menziesii* 196
 — × *multiflora* 192
 — *nipponica* 196
 — *opulifolia* **154, 155**
 — *prunifolia* 196
 — *thunbergii* 192, 196
 — *trilobata* 196
 — × *vanhouttei* **196, 197**
 — *veitchii* 196
Spiraea 8, 10
 — Blue **50, 51**
 — Garland 20, 22, 25
 — Vanhoutte's **196, 197**
Spiraea Bumalda hybrids 24, **194, 195**
St John's Wort 13, 24—26, **122, 123**
Staphylea 20
 — *bumalda* 198
 — *colchica* 198
 — × *elegans* 198
 — *pinnata* **198, 199**
Sumach, Stagshorn 12, 16, 20, 25, **174, 175**
 — Venetian **72, 73**
Symphoricarpos 16, 21—24
 — *albus* **200, 201**, 202

 — *albus* var. *rivularis* 201, 202
 — × *chenaultii* **202, 203**
 — *doorenbosii* 202
 — *hybrids* 202
 — *microphyllus* 202
 — *orbiculatus* 202
 — *racemosus* **200, 201**
 — *vulgaris* 202
Syringa 10, 13, 16, 19, 20, 22
 — × *chinensis* **204, 205**
 — *josikaea* 204
 — *reflexa* 204
 — *vulgaris* 204, 207
Syringa Vulgaris Hybrids **206, 207**

Tamarisk 20, **208, 209**
Tamarix 20
 — *parviflora* 208
 — *pentandra* 208
 — *tetrandra* **208, 209**
Tilia 23
Tulip Tree **136, 137**
Tutsan 122

Ulmus 7

Viburnum 22, 26
 — × *burkwoodii* 212
 — × *carlcephalum* 212
 — *carlesii* 24—26, 212
 — *farreri* **210, 211**
 — *farreri candidissimum* 211
 — *fragrans* **210, 211**
 — *lantana* **212, 213**
 — *macrocephalum* 212
 — *opulus* **214, 215**
 — *sargentii* 212
 — *utile* 212
Viburnum 9, 10, 13, 16, 21
 — Fragrant 20
 — Winter-flowering **210, 211**
Vinca 24

Wayfaring Tree **212, 213**
Weigela florida **216, 217**
 — *japonica* 218
 — *praecox* 218
 — *rosea* **216, 217**
Weigela 13, 20, **216, 217**
 — Hybrids 22, **218, 219**
Wig Tree **72, 73**
Willow 7
Witch Hazel 9, 10, 12—14
 — Chinese **110, 111**
 — Japanese 20, 22, **108, 109**
 — Ozark 112